# Grapevine

# Grapevine

## THE SPIRITUALITY OF GOSSIP

JERRY A. CAMERY-HOGGATT

FOREWORD BY SUSAN BIESECKER-MAST

Herald
Press

*Scottdale, Pennsylvania*
*Waterloo, Ontario*

**Library of Congress Cataloging-in-Publication Data**
Camery-Hoggatt, Jerry
Grapevine: the spirituality of gossip / Jerry A. Camery-Hoggatt.
p. cm.
Includes bibliographical references.
ISBN 0-8361-9196-X (pbk. : alk. paper)
1. Oral communication—Religious aspects—Christianity. 2. Gossip.
I. Title.
BV4597.53.C64 C36 2002
241'.672--dc21 2001006736

The paper used in this publication is recycled and meets the minimum requirements of American National Standard for Information Sciences—Permanence of Paper for Printed Library Materials, ANSI Z39.48-1984.


Library of Congress Catalog Card Number: 2001006736
International Standard Book Number: 0-8361-9196-X
Printed in the United States of America
Book and cover design by Merrill R. Miller

10 09 08 07 06 05 04 03 02 10 9 8 7 6 5 4 3 2 1

To order or request information, please call
1-800-759-4447 (individuals); 1-800-245-7894 (trade).
Website: www.mph.org

TO MY WIFE, SHALEEN,
WHO KEEPS ME SANE.

## CONTENTS

## FOREWORD

This book is based in two crucial premises. One is that the manner in which we "do church" is constitutive of the church. The other is that we "do church" through talk. Animated by these two premises, this book can teach all of us who seek to embody Christ on earth a great deal.

It is altogether too tempting, this book reminds us, for us to imagine that the church is what happens in a Sunday morning worship service, or what is proclaimed in a confession of faith, or what grows out of a commitment to mission. To be sure, these activities and statements by the church are formative of the church. They make the church what it is. Yet, there is something else that is making the church what it is everyday in the in-between times. In between the worship services, the collective statements, and the grand projects, there is talk. Talk, this book argues, is always making the church what it is. Depending on how we talk to one another, we make the church a body that is about inclusion or exclusion, suffering or redemption, pain or grace.

Taking talk seriously, as this book does, is not easy. One reason is that talk, by its very nature, is complicated. Another reason is that since we all talk so often and so much, we tend to think of it as a relatively simple matter. This book is right to challenge us to give more attention to our talk as an act of discipleship because of the power that talk exercises in shaping ourselves, the church, and the world.

Although taking talk seriously is not easy, reading this book surely is. This is so for a number of reasons, perhaps the most notable of which is its own use of talk. One of the most significant forms that our talk takes, as this book points out, is storytelling. In this book we encounter a thoroughly enjoyable and profound kind of storytelling. To my mind, storytelling can do no better than to inspire us to make new meaning out of the complexities of our world. Again and again, this book does just that.

In story after story throughout this book we are brought into contact with some *other* that we imagine. As the story unfolds, we come to understand that other, and can think of a similar instance in our own lives where we encountered such an other. But through the telling of these stories we are invited to engage something we have missed before—the perspective or the meaning of that encounter for the other. In this way, this book gives us a glimpse into the rich, or dark, or beautiful, or troubled, or humorous aspects of the other we failed to see through the meaning we had imposed. Importantly, such revelation is not limited to the other person but also applies to the other within. Through these stories we too are invited to engage the other within us that we do not know.

This book does not offer simple answers though it does provide us with helpful guidance. Most importantly, it inspires us to work toward a manner of talk that promises grace, joy, and peace. As disciples of Christ, we cannot pass up this important teaching.

—*Susan Biesecker-Mast*
*Professor of Communications, Bluffton College*

# PREFACE

*We live in narrative, we live in story. Existence has a story shape to it. We have a beginning and an end, we have a plot, we have character.*
—Eugene Peterson

In the book, *Small Decencies,* human resources consultant John Cowan describes a moment of personal dismay after a weekend workshop with a group of upper-level management trainees. "I never wanted to run another training course," he says, "carefully taking managers through the facets of leadership, giving them feedback collected from their peers and reports, patiently discussing what they might do about it only, in all likelihood, to have them forget it."[1]

Such a realization was dismaying to Cowan because of what it implied about the meaning of his whole life's work, and before he went home he nursed his discouragement with a long walk by the river. It happens that this event took place in the same city as the seminary where years before he had trained for the priesthood, and the walk along the river brought him to the seminary grounds. There on the grounds of the seminary was a series of walls that he himself had constructed many years before during a summer recess. *Now there's one thing you accomplished in your life that nobody can deny*, he thought. But then: *Three abandoned walls do not a satisfying career make.*

In the end, the walls didn't comfort Cowan, but they did provide an answer to the problem of meaning he faced. "I realized that I did not build them. *We* built them." The walls weren't built by one man, but by a team of men working together. In the same way, Cowan thought, his personal contribution to the world of human resources only finds its true meaning as part of the whole range of transformations that have taken place in the world of work. Before human resources began as a field of research, management decisions were always made from above, people dressed and acted alike, boardrooms were dominated by men, and those men had very little meaningful life outside the workplace. Now, looking back, all of that is different. The working world is more open-ended, more fluid; the management of power and the processes of decision making are more cooperative; a collaborative spirit is more the norm than the exception. Women are a more visible and more important presence than ever before.

> I have been but a drop in the stream. But as a drop I have made a difference. . . . I offer this salute to all of us who are drops in the stream. My cause has been the humanization of work. Yours might be some technology or task. Together we can take immense pride in the last twenty-five years. We have done much. . . . Most of us should be warned that only the exceptional few can point to their own dramatic effect on history. But we, the unexceptional many, can take much credit for what we have done to push the stream along.[2]

What Cowan is doing in this momentary reflection is "making meaning"—in this case defining the significance of his career by connecting it up with a wider story, a larger whole.

People have made such connections throughout history. Social scientists, psychologists, and theologians call these large, epic stories *meta-narratives*. Meta-narratives are those huge, encompassing stories in which our smaller individual stories find a place. America Goes West and the Civil Rights Movement are meta-narratives. Perhaps the most significant and most telling for Christians is the way people have connected their individual plots to the story of redemption as it is portrayed in the Bible and interpreted in the life of the church.

There's a lot of anxious talk these days about the decline of the meta-narratives in our culture. Without the grand stories, so the argument goes, we don't know who we are. In this book I offer another view, one that is both more hopeful and more cautionary. Here I am concerned about the *micro-narratives* that are packaged in the daily conversations around the water cooler, in the coffee shop, on the porch, at the dinner table. These tiny stories—sometimes no longer than a few short sentences—can have a cumulative effect on our private experience that far outweighs the mass effect of the meta-narratives of the culture in general. This book is about daily gossip.

Unlike the meta-narratives, the stories generated in the daily gossip are small and quick. Like moths, they flit into existence for a few moments, and then just as quickly grow tired and die, replaced by a new generation that may last no longer. Whatever fate the meta-narratives are experiencing, the micro-narratives are doing well. This is, I think, a reflection of the fact that human beings are inveterate meaning makers. We can't help ourselves. We're going to talk, and when we talk, we interpret, and when we interpret we make meaning. Because we make meaning through *talk,* and because the talk connects us to one another, we will always make meaning in this way.

More specifically, this book is about the role the daily talk plays in the ways we form our ideas about the world, about ourselves, and about God. Gossip comes and goes, but before it leaves it can permanently mark our spiritual lives—for good or for ill. My intention here is to take the talk seriously as a topic for psychological and theological reflection. Gossip plays an important role in our ongoing effort to come to terms with the challenges of life; it's how we find our way, and sometimes how we lose it.

Before we begin, a word about terms: I intend to use the word *gossip* in its older and more generous sense. Several years ago I was asked to speak on this topic for a local call-in radio show. The host of the program, who had not heard what I have to say about gossip, and assuming that I would condemn it outright, introduced me by saying that I was going to talk about "the sin we never talk about." It was a wildly funny time as I explored with her why we could not be the people of God unless we commit "the sin we never talk about."

There are three reasons I don't intend to disparage this universal human activity. The first is that it has only been in the last hundred years or so that talking about community news has gotten such a bad rap. When the talk show host used the word *gossip,* what she meant was *malicious gossip.* In its earlier life, the term derived from two Old English words, *god*, meaning "good," and *sibb*, meaning "family relationship." *Godsibb* referred not to the talk, but to the deep sense of connection—the brotherhood—that comes from shared knowledge, shared histories, shared interests, shared *news.* Etymologically, the term is related to the word *gospel.* In this book I preserve that larger meaning. The intentions of gossip are as often positive as they are negative. In a recent study (conducted, by the way, by a process I do find objectionable, eavesdropping) researchers at Northeastern University found that the conversation in the university's dorm lounges was clearly negative or malicious only 27 percent of the time. And it was clearly positive 27 percent of the time. The rest of the time the conversation ranged in a kind of mixed evaluation.[3]

The second reason I want to preserve a larger meaning is that positive intentions do not always yield positive consequences, nor do negative intentions always yield negative consequences. If the members of the football squad stand around after practice talking admiringly about the team captain's sexual exploits, their admiration may be genuine and their intentions toward the captain entirely positive, but with each example they reinforce a negative and demeaning morality.

The churches in which I was raised were all small Pentecostal congregations, peopled almost entirely by blue-collar workers. These were God-fearing, hardworking, simple people. The theology that mattered to them was not the systematic kind I teach in university, but the simple exchange of testimonies about the times God had somehow been there for them when they needed help the most. Some of the stories they told were rough, chiseled from the concrete of hard work, broken marriages, drugs, and in some cases, violence. They were stories hard on plot and character, stories with the packaging already broken, markdown table stories. They were stories of triumph, of loss, of emerging hope; stories of the power of God. Yet, they were powerful stories of judgment and grace. For all their jagged edges, they were grace-full stories.

I cannot tell you how deeply I respect these people, who passed their faith to me in so many intangible ways. The men and women of the churches in which I grew up are still heroes to me. But it was such people, too, who with absolutely good intentions told me stories designed to turn me away from going to college, and after that from seminary, and after that, university. "What will happen if the Lord comes back and finds you wasting your time in a place like that?" they wanted to know. They told me about ministerial students who had "lost their souls at Bible College" because they had been forced to read "liberal" theology. Their arguments rested on the importance of reading the Bible *simply*: "The Bible was written for simple people, common people, and the more you study, the less you will be able to understand it." In the end, they just offered warnings: "Those people down there know enough to destroy your faith!" Good intentions do not always lead to good consequences.

On the other hand, even malicious gossip may have positive consequences. If members of a church share with each other the news that Susie Smith is sleeping with her college boyfriend, their conscious intentions may be good; their subconscious intentions may be self-protective or self-aggrandizing. The direct effect on Susie Smith may be disastrous, and the indirect effect on the children—who are overhearing it all—may be a graphic lesson that Christians do not do such things. Years later, those same children may turn down their own boyfriends' advances for fear of being ground up in the gossip mill. Fear of being talked about may be a positive thing if it bolsters them when their own internalized morality is being stretched to the point of tearing. Then again, if things go awry, they may lose all hope of ever measuring up to gossip's strictures, and leave the faith altogether. Often the bad and the good are like the weeds and the wheat, impossible to disentangle completely, requiring the perspective of a later judgment and the insight of a wiser and more omniscient judge.[4]

At the very least, gossip is a way of taking a public position, of stepping out, of saying out loud that there is a right and there is a wrong. In *Moralities of Everyday Life*, John Sabini and Maury Silver state this as a principle:

> Gossip brings ethics home by introducing abstract morality to the mundane. . . . Gossip then is a mechanism of social control in that it allows individuals to express, articulate, and commit themselves to a moral position in the act of talking about someone. . . . It is a way that we come to know what our own evaluations really are. . . . [It] is a training ground for both self-clarification and public moral action.[5]

The third reason I do not intend to disparage gossip in this book is that it is one of the important ways we have of connecting with each other, tuning in to one another's hurts, fears, hopes, and dreams. To paraphrase Deborah Tannen's helpful phrase, *rapport-talk as lament*, gossip is a way of praisin' the Lord and singin' the blues . . . over the back fence. Where would we be if we could not do that? Not all water cooler talk is sinful talk; some is actually healing and redemptive. Tex Sample has it right: "The point is not to eliminate gossip—an unlikely possibility—but to encourage its positive use."[6]

Finally, a word of thanks to those who have contributed their time and wisdom to this project. These include colleagues, students, and friends: Meg Alton, Rebecca Johnson, Roger Johnson, John Kinsky, Jason Lamoreaux, Jeff Lethcoe, Markita Roberson, Stephen Rose, Lydia Sarandon, and Peter St. Don. If you take exception to what you read here, please don't blame them; they did the best they could with me.

CHAPTER ONE

# THE GOD OF THE GRAPEVINE

## Praisin' the Lord and Singin' the Blues . . . Over the Back Fence

*Conduct and character are largely determined by the nature of the words we currently use to discuss ourselves and the world around us.*
—Aldous Huxley

In August 1968, philosopher E. F. Schumacher paid a tourist visit to Leningrad, Russia. To find his way around he consulted one of the official maps of the city. What puzzled him was that the map showed several churches, but omitted others. Several enormous churches were visible right before his eyes but were missing from the map. He asked an interpreter for an explanation.

"We don't show churches on our maps."

Schumacher indicated one that was clearly marked on the map.

"That is a museum," said the interpreter, "not what we call a 'living church.' It is only the 'living churches' that we don't show."

Schumacher's comment on this little exchange has large implications for the ways we learn and teach about the world:

> It then occurred to me that this was not the first time I had been given a map which failed to show many things I could see right in front of my eyes. All through school and university I had been given maps and knowledge on which there was hardly a trace of many of the things that I most cared about and that seemed to me to be of the greatest possible importance to the conduct of my life.[1]

This book is about two such omissions from our normal thinking about Christian spirituality. The first is gossip and the profound effects gossip can have on our understanding of what it means to be Christian. The second is the reality, that like everybody else, Christians struggle to come to terms with dimensions of our inner lives that may trouble us very deeply, that bring us shame or confusion, and that above all else we know we have to keep secret. These two landmarks of our inner lives are so closely connected that one cannot be properly understood without the other. When either one is missing from our maps of the spiritual life, we can lose our way without being aware of it. Whatever else it is, the practice of spirituality within the Christian tradition is a particular way of coming to terms with our secret selves.

Imagine for a moment that you could sit down with the pastoral staff of any large church and pose for them the following question: What single factor has the largest influence on the spiritual life of your congregation? Human nature being what it is, each of the pastors is likely to name something from his or her own area of responsibility.

The senior pastor will say, "the preaching." It is, after all, the preaching that spearheads the way the Bible is interpreted, and the preaching that models the way the congregation will engage in its own Bible study. Or the parish priest might say, "the celebration of the mass," because within the mass we encounter the mystery of the eucharist or the reality of grace.

The music minister will say either, "the hymns," or "the worship choruses." In fact, there is a minor war raging in the choir rooms of America between traditionalists, who miss the hymns, and the leaders of worship teams, who advocate the new seeker-friendly style of worship. When the traditionalists state their case, it usually runs like this: "The old hymns are important for their theological substance. It's from the hymns that people learn their basic theology."

Advocates of seeker-friendly worship point out that the diction of the hymns can be off-putting, while the music is old and staid; some would say stale. What is needed instead is an upbeat style of music that leads people easily into the experience of worship—"because worship has the power to transform the soul." Seeker-friendly worship tends to be trendy and accessible, with choruses, not hymns. Theology can be learned later, in Bible study groups.

The Christian education director would agree with the music minister on this last point, but would reverse the sequence: "What shapes the spiritual life of the church is study, or at least training in the basic concepts of the faith. At the core of the spirituality of the church are Bible studies, special topics, and guest speakers."

The youth minister would agree, but would add the category: ministry trips. The spiritual life of the church is shaped by summer camps, small-group ministries, and trips to the inner city. For all of his or her focus on the moment, it is the youth minister who holds the longest perspective: The youth of today are the church of tomorrow. Investment in youth may not yield a return for decades, and yet, "only those who are mature will plant a tree under which they know they will never sit." The spirituality of the church of today is the harvest of the work of youth pastors twenty years ago, but that harvest is unnoticed because the workers themselves have left the field and become senior pastors—who now believe that the spiritual life of the church is shaped by the preaching!

## But What of the Sermons We Hear at the Water Cooler?

This book is based on the observation that if we could add all of this work together into a heap, and somehow find a way to measure it, we would discover that all of it together does not have as large an impact on the spirituality of the church as what we say to one another and about one another in the church foyer, at the water cooler, and over our cups of coffee.

Suppose the senior pastor preaches a fine sermon on the need for racial reconciliation in her troubled parish. The final impact of the sermon is much later, at the dinner table, long after the service of worship is over and everyone has gone home. Mom and Dad may discuss the sermon's main points and what challenges it holds for them and their family. The children overhear the discussion and learn, among other things, how to listen to sermons, and whether or not their family is going to dismiss this one as irrelevant! Or maybe they talk about the fact that the preacher is a woman, and what right has she to stand behind a pulpit anyway? If they do, they teach their children exactly what they think about the proper place of women in the church. Or perhaps they don't discuss the sermon at all, but instead they focus the dinner conversation on the latest football scores. In that silence they may be teaching their children the unintended lesson that sermons should be kept in their place—in the sanctuary—and not dragged out into real life.

The youth go on a mission trip, but it's what they say later to their friends about the trip that establishes its final impact. Recently my teenage daughter Brynn came home from a trip to Mexico. While she was there she had shared some candy with a young Mexican girl named Marisa. As Brynn watched, Marisa broke the candy into three pieces, ate one and put the other two in her pocket. Why did she do that? Because she had two brothers, she said, and she was saving the candy for them. "And they didn't know!" Brynn said to us. "She could have eaten it, and they would never have known!" As she has told and retold this little story, Marisa's tiny gesture of human generosity has come to symbolize for Brynn the meaning of her trip. We could tell that she was humbled and challenged by it, and that by sharing her story with us she was also telling us that she was changed in some small but significant way.

The point here is not that the event happened, but that in *telling the story about the event*, Brynn preserved it, internalized it, and owned it as her own. She also replicated it for her family. I wasn't there, but I too have been humbled and challenged by this tiny act of generosity. Each time Brynn tells the story she magnifies the event and clarifies its meaning. By telling her story in one way and not another, Brynn was also being changed in small but significant ways. When she says aloud what she thinks about this or that, she declares herself. She takes a public position from which she can back out only awkwardly. The telling and retelling consolidate and solidify her position.

Storytelling is also a group thing. Brynn can hardly tell her story without an audience to listen, and the reactions of the people listening shape the way she tells it. Even learning what *not* to tell is an important factor in her spiritual development. As Brynn grows she will learn who ought not to know certain things, who can be trusted to keep confidences, who will tell her secrets out of school. These are important pieces of the puzzle of daily life, and the way she assembles them will shape important dimensions of her spiritual outlook as well. What she chooses to include, what she chooses to leave out, whom she tells, and in what contexts—all of these together represent activities of spiritual formation.

## Whatever Else, We're Going to Talk

Brynn's experience illustrates an important but neglected dimension of spiritual formation: The intensity of the talk—its direction of movement, what it condemns and what it affirms—profoundly shapes our spiritual lives. And yet we can hardly do without the talk. There are certain things we must do if we are to be the church, and many of those things we cannot do if we do not talk about the church's daily life. There are three further reasons why this is so.

First, we do not come as blank books to our understanding of the spiritual life. Pastors and Bible teachers cannot simply write on us whatever they will. Instead, we come already formed by ideas about what it means to be Christian, what it means to study the Bible, what it means to be witnesses in the workplace. Whenever we learn anything new we do so by connecting the new information to the network of things we already know. Where did that prior information come from? Largely from the daily conversation that makes up the life of the families, churches, and communities in which we were raised.

Second, for all of its self-talk about being the people of the Book, the church primarily carries on its business as an oral enterprise, rather than as an enterprise of print. In a recent discussion entitled *Ministry in an Oral Culture*, Tex Sample points out that when oral people learn something new, they tend to start with practice and then work outward to more general understanding. That is, they learn by apprenticeship rather than by theory.[2] Apprenticeship is basically an ongoing conversation between a teacher and a student who work together and talk together. It has a certain randomness about it. Problems are encountered and addressed as they occur, rather than as part of a systematic and comprehensive curriculum.

Apprenticeship isn't a bad way to learn. Recently I had some construction work done on my house. My carpenter, Jerry, brought along his thirteen-year-old son, Anthony. "My own father taught me how to work," Jerry said to me, "and I intend to teach Anthony. Because if I don't, who will?" As they worked, he gave Anthony little jobs to do that would help him master his tools. He checked his work. He answered questions. He made him tear out some of the work and do it over again. Anthony left one step closer to becoming a carpenter in his own right. That's how apprenticeship works its way. Because problems are raised as they occur in practice, the learner can see them firsthand, and can watch the way they're resolved in real life. According to Sample, apprentices generally don't take notes, they don't make outlines, and they don't *do critique.* What they learn, they learn as needed, concretely, with calluses on the hands, successes right there where they can be seen by everybody, and failed attempts carried out at the end of the day and put in the trash bin—none of the abstractions of theory here. In the same way, what we do learn about God on the grapevine has a certain immediacy about it; it somehow just *feels* more real. None of the abstractions of theory here, either.

The third reason we learn about God on the grapevine is that we have to find ways of going beyond studying the Bible to being people of genuine faith who live out their faith in the modern world, in real life. This poses a problem of its own. The Bible was written in a world that was profoundly different from ours. In order to be "biblical" people in a secular and modern world, we must somehow learn to apply the truth of Scripture to circumstances the writers of Scripture would have found puzzling, perhaps even bizarre. Is it even possible to speak of a biblical position on, say, the bomb, or AIDS, or heart-lung transplants, or the growing presence of postmodern ideas in the world's university system?

There must be some way to bridge the gaps between the ancient world and the modern one, between theory and practice, between what we say to one another on Sunday in worship and what we do to one another on Monday. Such bridges are constructed of large bodies of information that is held loosely and tacitly just outside of the interpreter's conscious thought. We face similar problems in other areas of life. In a recent discussion of a parallel problem in the teaching of practical morality, social psychologists John Sabini and Maury Silver point out that this kind of information is often acquired through ordinary gossip:

> Principles are as important to morality, the social order, as they are to law or physics. But the skill in law and the skill in physics lie not so much in learning the rules as in acquiring the tacit knowledge to apply them.
>
> You've been *taught* not to bother the neighbors, and you've been *trained* to recognize what counts as bothering the neighbors: playing music too loud after 11:00 p.m. or riding motorcycles without mufflers at night. But now you've moved into a new graduate student apartment complex with very thin walls and a neighbor, studying for her Ph.D. qualifying exams. She finds your normal sound disruptive of her studying. Your socialized rule that you shouldn't bother the neighbors wasn't applied for you to this new circumstance. Of course, you have principles. . . .
>
> Here, gossip can be of help. . . . If you've been lucky enough to participate, even as a listener, in gossip with other students with thin walls and noisy or nervous neighbors, you may have picked up some specific examples of excessive noise and reasonable lives. And these specifics, like settled cases in common law, can serve as precedents for your construction of a reasonable solution.[3]

This is just like the problem Christians face in the day-in-day-out business of being biblical people in a culture that the authors of the Bible would have found puzzling indeed. In the end, we must know something more than we can learn in Bible study, and that something more is often learned on the grapevine.

So it is, along with our Bible studies, sermons, hymns, and mission trips, that the fabric of church life is also woven from the tiny threads of thousands of moments around the water cooler and at the coffee shop. Every pastor or priest can tell you stories of how that fabric was frayed or torn because of the destructive effects of gossip and innuendo. A young woman, prominent in the youth group, makes a terrible mistake of judgment and finds herself pregnant and unmarried. The thread pickers in the congregation can completely unravel her place in the weaving. That may be important for the group—to take a stand on such matters—but it can also be terribly destructive for her.

But the talk can also be redemptive. Instead of talking about what is wrong with her, the church might ask what can be done to help. A young mother gets cancer and the care-giving arm of the church comes to her aid. The telephone lines buzz the news, and as the members of her congregation pray for her and talk among themselves about how she's doing, thousands of tiny moments of spiritual formation take place.

**The Talk Brings the Sermon to the Street**

It may seem a bit odd for a Christian theologian to talk about spirituality this way. Our maps of the spiritual life tend to focus on prayer, testimony, the sacraments, fellowship with other Christians, Bible study, times of spiritual retreat, or—in the tradition in which I was reared—camp meetings and revivals. It somehow seems more normal to have maps of spirituality that highlight what we do in church and leave everything else out.[4] We come to believe that spirituality is one thing and daily life is something different altogether.

So I also believed. All of this changed abruptly for me one Sunday morning in church as I was preaching on the Lord's Prayer. I had read the text, and had begun my exposition. I do not remember how far along I was in my sermon when I said—and I still believe this—that "God is faithful to answer prayer." At that moment a woman in my congregation interrupted my sermon.

"And what exactly do you say . . ." she started out. (Suddenly everyone in the room was *present.*) "What do you say to an eight-year-old child who prays every night that her father will stop molesting her, and every night when she says her 'Amen,' her father comes in and does it again?"[5]

This woman's honest and searching challenge changed completely the kinds of questions I bring to my work as a pastor and as a theologian. I am convinced that when we compartmentalize reality in this way we end up seeing our religious lives *over against* the rest of life. We don't usually think of our workouts at the gym as spiritual activities, but they are. When a gang of young men beats up an old lady and steals her purse, that event has an effect on their spiritual lives. It is not a *non*spiritual act, but a *twisted* one. There's a spiritual dimension to the sniping we do at one another, the injustice collecting we do, or our attempts to justify our own actions or cover up our sense of inadequacy or shame. When we separate spirituality from the rest of life, we tend to treat God like a correction in the stock market—an inconvenience that brings everything back into line.

Most of us come by this tendency honestly. As a young man growing up in Pentecostal churches I often heard stories of how God had moved in some dramatic way—to heal a sick child, to save a broken marriage, or to make the mortgage payment just in the nick of time. The distinguishing characteristic of those stories was that the speaker was certain this was the hand of *God because there was no other explanation*. The sure sign of the power of God was its surprising way of disrupting the laws of nature! The conclusion I drew from all that talk was that where there was some other explanation, then surely God had kept out of the situation. At the center of my adolescent spirituality was an on-again-off-again God. God was always there when we had faith enough, and sometimes when the chips were down, but when things were going well we were pretty much on our own.

As an adult, I have rethought my on-again-off-again God, just as I have rethought my notion that the spiritual life is what we do in our worship services, Bible studies, and prayer meetings. Psychiatrist Carl Jung reportedly had this sign hanging on a wall near the door of his study: "Invited or not, God will be present." Surely he is right. We could not exclude God from the everyday world even if we wanted to. As I search for a spirituality that sees and responds to the divine thumbprints in daily life, I find myself listening more and more attentively for what sociologist Peter Berger once called "a rumor of angels."[6] To say that God uses ordinary events to accomplish divine purposes is to make the audacious suggestion that the Creator of the universe sometimes whispers to us over the back fence. And what God has to say to us in those whispered moments can echo much more deeply in the recesses of our inner lives than anything we might hear from the pulpit, in the hymns, on retreat, or on the ministry trips we plan for ourselves and our churches' youth.

If God uses ordinary means to accomplish divine purposes, we should not be surprised to find divine thumbprints on daily life. Sometimes even the ordinary exchanges of life represent God at work in an artful play for our souls. But this can be turned on its head: Such things as the communion of the saints—surely a divine accomplishment—is created in part by the ordinary structures of human social interaction. We turn to that matter in the next chapter.

CHAPTER TWO

# JOHN J. DUNBAR GOES INJUN

## Shibboleths, Taboos, and the Boundaries of the Church

*He drew a circle that shut me out—*
*Heretic, rebel, a thing to flout.*
*But love and I had the wit to win:*
*We drew a circle that took him in.*
—Edwin Markham

*After a little while the bystanders came up and said to Peter, "Certainly you are also one of them, for your accent betrays you."*
—Matthew 26:73

In the movie, *Dances with Wolves*, Lieutenant John Dunbar has been sent alone to the frontier to guard a long defunct military outpost named Fort Sedgewick. Inevitably, he encounters a tribe of Sioux Indians. The distrust is palpable in both directions, but eventually, through a series of chance encounters, it begins to break down. In time the Sioux accept him as a neighbor, then as a friend, and then as a member of their tribe. He learns the Sioux language and takes a wife, named Stands with a Fist, herself a white who was raised by the Sioux after a Pawnee attack had wiped out her parents' farm on the edge of the frontier. One of the most touching scenes in the film is the moment at which Stands with a Fist tells Dunbar that among the Sioux he is called by the name that provides the title for the film—Dances with Wolves.

In a particularly painful scene near the end of the movie, Dunbar has returned to his post to retrieve something of personal value, only to discover that the fort has been occupied by the United States army. The soldiers do not recognize that he is white, his horse is shot, he is captured and beaten, then taken to the stockade for interrogation. At first he speaks to his captors in English: "I am Lieutenant John J. Dunbar. This is my post. I came out from Fort Hayes last April but there was nobody here." Before the scene closes, however, he has learned that these men are enemies, and he shouts at them in Sioux: "I have nothing to say to you. You are not worth talking to. I am Dances with Wolves."

Perhaps more than any other, this scene drives home the point that John Dunbar has become a completely different person. It is significant that Dunbar, now Dances with Wolves, is still legally an officer in the United States Army, but the viewer in the audience knows that that is only a legal fiction now. The reason Dunbar is not Dunbar anymore, is that his primary loyalties have shifted dramatically. He has adopted an entirely different way of seeing the world, he takes entirely different things for granted, and he uses an entirely different language to talk about it all.

The transformation from Lieutenant John Dunbar to Dances with Wolves represents in a vivid and sweeping way all of the basic things that happen when we leave one social group and move to another. Even when we stay within a group, but somehow change our status, the same basic processes take place. This is so whether the group is a gang, a bridge party, a new team of workers in the field, or the church. Central to all of this is the language the members of the group speak when they're together. By this I mean not just their vocabulary and grammar, but also the habits of interpretation and the rhetorical structures exhibited and performed within the talk. These are the measures by which we decide what really happened and what did not; who our true allies are, and who are not; what's good, and what's not. We learn these things through tiny, sometimes barely perceptible habits of the daily gossip.

## The Gossip Determines Who's In . . . And Who's Out

When I was a young boy the chiefs of our neighborhood tribe were two brothers named Bill and Jerry Roskilly. It didn't take us long after we moved to the neighborhood to learn that the Roskilly house was the working center of the tribe's universe. It was where base camp was, the place where the war councils were held. All the wandering and raiding, all the whooping and hollering, somehow started and ended *there.* We also learned that the Roskilly brothers were themselves a repository of real, genuine, nearly magical power—more so even than our mother. They had the power to create, just as they had the power to destroy. They were more than chiefs; they were *medicine men.* That was because Bill and Jerry Roskilly were the gatekeepers of the tribal language. They were the ones who made up all of the slang, or decided who else could add a word or a phrase to the neighborhood patois.

More importantly, Bill and Jerry were also the only ones in the group who could give anyone else a nickname and make it stick. One summer they decided that everyone's given names should end with the sound, "*a-bru,*" pronounced like "*a bru*-nette," only a little shorter and heavier on the final syllable. Bill became "*Bill-a-bru.*" My older brother John became "*John-a-bru,*" and my other brother Jim, who had already been dubbed "*Jaymus,*" became "*Jaymus-a-bru.*" But when it came to "*Jerr-a-bru,*" we had a problem. Jerry Roskilly already had that name, so there was nothing left for me. I was left as just "Jerry," and never received a nickname.

It was the loneliest summer of my childhood.

I was never included in the war councils, and I had to be "It" if I wanted to play hide-and-seek and kick-the-can. My mother saw all of this happening, but she was virtually powerless to do anything about it. She tried hard enough. She gave my brothers strict instructions not to ride their bikes faster than I could ride mine, she told them they couldn't go swim in the Roskillys' swimming pool unless I went too, and she insisted that the gang should play at our house sometimes. She even gave me a nickname of her own—she called me Jedidiah—but that only made it clearer to me and everyone else that the Roskillys had not done the same.

As powerful as my mother was, she was powerless even to enter the social territory of our childhood. An invisible boundary stood like an invisible sign over the door of the invisible clubhouse—"No grown-ups allowed." As an outsider, she could not *invite* me in. She could *require* that I be treated like a member of the gang, and she could impose serious consequences when my brothers did not do so, just as the United States army could impose consequences on Lieutenant John J. Dunbar, but when membership is achieved by coercion, when it is not matched by the invitation of insiders, it serves only to deepen a person's sense of being left out. In the end, my mother couldn't do the one thing that was necessary if I was to become a real insider—she couldn't assign me a nickname and make it stick with the neighborhood gang.

I have had similar experiences as an adult. One can become an official member of almost any group. The churches I know are almost universally eager for new members. Potential converts are courted and witnessed to, put on mailing lists, and receive calls from officially designated contact persons. But the conditions for membership and the conditions for becoming insiders can be quite different. It's like attending a concert. Anyone can buy a ticket, but you have to know someone to be invited backstage. In general, this is a good thing, so long as the conditions set for becoming insiders are the right ones. Sometimes those conditions are hostile to the gospel, and it may take a movement of grace and moral courage to reach across the boundary and draw someone in.

Homiletics professor Fred Craddock tells a story about a conversation he once had with an old man while he was on vacation in the Smokey Mountains of Tennessee. The old man had interrupted Craddock's dinner, very much uninvited, and had persisted in pushing the conversation beyond Craddock's comfort zone. In the following dialogue, the old man speaks first:

"Evening."

"Evening."

"You all on vacation?"

"Yessir."

"Goin' to be here long?"

"Won't be here but a week."

"Well, I hope you have a good time. What do you do?"

"I teach in seminary."

"Oh. You a preacher?"

"Well, yeah."

"I want to tell you a story."

"Well . . . have a seat at our table here."

"I was born back here in these mountains. My mother was not married. Such shame. And when we went to town the other women looked at her and looked at me and began to guess who I was and who my father was, and the reproach that was hers fell upon me. And it was painful. At school the children had a name for me. I hid in the weeds at recess. I ate my lunch alone. I started going to a little church back in there called Laurel Springs. There was a preacher, a craggy rough preacher. Prince Albert coat. Beard. Big voice. He scared me, but he fascinated me. I would go just for the sermon. I was afraid somebody would speak to me in the earlier part and say, 'What's a boy like you doin' in church?' And I was afraid. One Sunday after I'd been goin' for some time, some of the people queued up in the aisle, and I couldn't rush out as I usually did. I couldn't get by. I began to chill. Somebody will say something to me. I need to get out of here. I felt a hand on my shoulder and I looked out of the corner of my eye, and it was that preacher. I saw his beard, and I saw that face, and I thought, 'Oh, no.' That preacher looked at me and said, 'Well, boy. Boy, you're a child of . . .' He paused, and I thought, 'Oh, no.' He said, 'Boy, you're a child of . . . God. I see a striking resemblance.' He swatted me on the bottom and said, 'Go claim your inheritance.' "

At this point Craddock interrupted the old man: "What's your name?"

"Ben Hooper."

"Ben Hooper? Ben Hooper! Oh, yes. I seem to remember my father telling me about the people of Tennessee twice electing a governor named Ben Hooper."

Craddock's final comment serves as a wonderful frame around this little dialogue: "He told me a story. No, no, no. He told me *the* Story."[1]

Ben Hooper's is even better: "I was born that day."

Boundaries are important lest we lose our identity, but the wrong boundaries can be tools of the devil.

### The Gossip Hardens the Boundaries

Pushing on boundaries from the outside can make them more rigid. Clearly this is what happened with the Roskillys. What my mother didn't realize was that the pressure she was placing from the outside was the basic topic of discussion at the Roskilly war councils—I learned this later. The harder she pushed, the louder and more frenzied the war drums beat. Once years ago in class, one of my sociology professors at university, Peter Berger, explained this as a principle of group dynamics:

> What happens when a social group perceives itself to be under threat? (Whether or not it actually *is* under threat is

irrelevant, he said. What matters is the *perception* of threat.) When a social group perceives itself to be under threat it finds ways of consolidating its boundaries, and the greater the sense of threat, the more arbitrary the boundary marking.

The earliest and most influential social scientist to explore the role of language in establishing social group boundaries was Edward Sapir. Sapir pointed out that there is an almost universal tendency of social groups to develop their own tiny dialects and mini-languages.[2] Perhaps the commonest place where such things happen is in families. Lots of families (I suspect most *healthy* families) have odd little dialects that they use among themselves. In my family, raisins are *onies,* ice cream is *icee c'doom*, and my friend Roger is called *Gooch*. According to Sapir, these little family languages are part of the psychological and social apparatus that tells us that we fit here, that we're members, that we *belong*. More importantly, the dialects form little fences around the family, and in that way they help the family survive. I can imagine families that do not have family languages, I even know some, but I wouldn't want to be part of one.

The Bible tells of a similar use of language to distinguish insiders from outsiders. The Gileadites had taken the fords of the Jordan, which they held against their enemies the Ephraimites. Possession of the ford gave them control over the movements of men and troops. Whenever Ephraimite refugees, posing as Gileadites, tried to use the ford they were unmasked by a simple linguistic test: "Pronounce the word *shibboleth*." But the Ephraimites could not pronounce the word, stumbling over the opening "s" sound. When caught, they were butchered on the spot (Judges 12:5-7).

Other kinds of groups have their own private insiders' languages, too, which clearly serve as modern-day shibboleths in the determination of group boundaries. I attended Gordon-Conwell Theological Seminary in Hamilton,

Massachusetts, thirty miles north of Boston. From the minute I moved there I was fascinated by the way the New Englanders talk. On one level, the talk forms one of the critical boundary markers by which local people distinguish local people—called *townies*—from outsiders—who are either *summer folk* or simply *from away*. North of Hamilton is a town named Ipswich. Hamilton townies never say, "Let's go *up* to Ipswich"; they always say, "Let's go *over* to Ipswich." (Actually, they say, "O*vah* to Ipswich." Correct pronunciation counts, too.) This is a tiny little boundary marker, and one that's essentially invisible to an outsider. Tell a townie that you're "going up to Ipswich," and you also tell her you're from away, that you're not one of them. Based on that clue alone, she may hold back from telling you any of the tidbits of information only townies are allowed to know. (The use of the feminine pronouns here, instead of the older, "him" and "he" is yet another indication of a modern-day shibboleth.)

The language barrier between insiders and outsiders can easily become elitist. Diction and vocabulary don't just tell townies who the outsiders are, they give the townies a kind of leverage, a way of managing power. A famous study of the ways languages change over time found that locals on Martha's Vineyard—who know themselves as *islanders*—actually adopted cruder patterns of speech to distinguish themselves from the increasingly invasive presence of the *off-islanders*, who were building estates on the island. Off-islanders, after all, are Ivy League educated and wealthy. Debasing the island's local diction was a subtle but effective form of elitism, a way of looking down on someone from below.[3]

## The Gossip Tells Us What We Can Say . . . and What We Can't

On the other side of this coin is our penchant for imposing taboo restrictions on language as another way of marking and reinforcing boundaries around the group. Taboo is what you're *not* allowed to do or say if you want to be part of the family. Recently I told a class of students about taboo, and we had a long and fruitful discussion of how taboo language—and taboo practices—works in the ordinary life of the church.

After class one of the students told me that she had been at a baptismal service the preceding week. One particular baptism stood out to her as remarkable. She took pains to make it clear that the baptismal candidate was still new in the faith—very new. He was "just saved the day before," he was "a brand new baby Christian," he was a street person who had never set foot in a church before. All he knew was that he had found Jesus, or Jesus had found him, and that he was new in Christ. But his language patterns were still those of "the old man."

"As he came up out of the water," she said, "he was beaming. He looked at us all and said, 'I'm so f—ing happy in Jesus!'" Fortunately, the church in this case was as forgiving as Jesus was, and this outburst—which might have gotten him drowned in some congregations—was met with redemptive laughter and hearty smiles.

It's probably significant that she told me this story after class. She watched me closely to see if I would flinch. The fact that I didn't, the fact that I have chosen to tell it here, and the diction with which I have told it, all signal to you something of the nature of my own spirituality. The reaction you have to the telling, if I could see it, would tell me a lot about yours.

## The Gossip Tells Us What We Can *Do* . . . And What We'd Better Not

Taboo can also involve objectionable practices. Recently one of my graduate students brought me a gift—an empty Maccabee beer bottle. The Maccabees were a group of Jewish guerilla fighters in the second century B.C. When this student told me confidentially that he knew where one could buy beer named after the Maccabees, I suddenly needed an empty bottle as a prop in a story I tell. He promised to help me out. He was careful to empty it before he brought it on campus, surely as a service to me. When he got to my office, he pulled it out of his shirtsleeve, where he had hidden it from view. Drinking beer, even beer named after ancient Jewish war heroes, is taboo on our campus.

The fact that he provided this service for me marks a tentative but significant change in our relationship. I have not asked him how he found out about Maccabee beer. Or what it tastes like. If the dean of students should hear this story, he might very well ask me who the student was. The dean has that right—it's part of his job—but I won't tell him. To do that would be to damage the tiny but significant social boundary marker the student and I have set up. This is important: His gift of a beer bottle and my reception of it do not merely signal a new level of trust between us, they make that level of trust possible.

Taboo can mean more than just forbidden words, phrases, and practices. It can also involve forbidden opinions, points of view, and attitudes. Suppose for a moment that you were sexually active in high school. Perhaps you also shared stories of your conquests with the others in the gym. You shape your talk in the locker room to bolster your reputation in the parking lot: "I can tell you, Susie isn't easy, but boy is she worth it! Way better than Helen. But Helen wasn't my first, you know, not by a long shot."

Now suppose that sometime during your freshman year at college you come into Christian faith, but you don't make any significant change in your language. You get up one night in Bible study and give your testimony: "I really like getting it on with high school girls. It makes you feel alive, the conquest. You know what I mean? What a great time!" Will you be asked to speak again? Hardly!

Instead, you retell your past history from the point of

view of your new commitment to Christ: "In high school, I was running from the Lord and I didn't even know it." On a theological level, your salvation involves making a confession of faith in Jesus, but if you want to join the church, you have to change the way you talk. Be transformed by the renewing of your mind, the Bible says. God looks on the heart, it says, but the church looks for evidence of that transformation in the renewing of your vocabulary.

Even the taboo boundaries surrounding gossip itself have to be learned—and where better to learn them than in the exchange of gossip? In a short tongue-in-cheek essay, authors Judi Culbertson and Patti Bard explain "How to Find Out the Latest Without Resorting to Idle Gossip." The perfect solution is to play "Let's All Pray for Poor Mrs. Jensen."[4] The single rule about LAPFPMJ is that you must give precise and accurate details, so everyone can "pray intelligently."

## The Gossip Tells Us Who We'd Better Not Cross . . . and Why

This matter of taboo raises the twin issues of social norms, and the sanctions leveled against any who violate those norms. When Dances with Wolves is arrested by the army and taken to the stockade, his interrogators repeat a single question over and over again: "Why are you out of uniform?" The fact that he refuses even to acknowledge their question violates another norm. Their decision to send him to Fort Hayes for court marshal and hanging is nothing personal, either, but is intended to make a public example of him. The hanging of John Dunbar is primarily a strategy of social control precisely because it will be talked about among the other men. This is what the army does to anyone who "turns Injun."

What is accomplished *formally* through court marshal and hanging happens *informally* through the grapevine all the time. Gossip is a play of power more than a way of passing along information. Anyone who has been the victim of malicious gossip knows what it's like to be tried and hanged in the court of public opinion.

### The Gossip Connects Us with Our Past . . . And with Our Future

Like other forms of storytelling, gossip also tells us who we are by connecting us with our past, or rather, by allowing us to take ownership of a past, even if it was not our own. When we become naturalized citizens of the United States, we may find ourselves reciting the details of American history as though our people were there all along: "Fourscore and seven years ago, *our* fathers brought forth on this continent, a new nation."

A deep psychological and emotional connection with one's past is an important part of coming to terms with the present, and after that the future. When my parents were divorced my father returned to his hometown in Oklahoma, "to put my life back in order," he said. There he found and married a childhood sweetheart. Dorothy, my stepmother, has told us story after story about my father's childhood, and in the stories I have come to understand a little better the forces that made him the man he is. Dorothy's stories helped me view my father through a more compassionate and forgiving lens, and ultimately to see him as a thoughtful and courageous human being. In reconnecting with my father, I have also somehow reconnected with parts of myself that had been buried in the rubble of my grief and anger at him for what I experienced as unfair treatment as a child.

### The Gossip Forces Us to Declare Our Loyalties

In the end, it isn't just what is said to us, but our *take* on what is said that matters. We hear a story and we take a position—pro, or con, or indifference. That position may call for action—anger, compassion, silence, prayer, or perhaps just delaying as we await further clues. Sometimes we define ourselves *over against* the norms expressed in the gossip; we stand with our backs to the prevailing social and psychological winds. As we respond to those challenges, as we take up our positions, as we risk alienation or decide where we are willing to cut a deal, we clarify the boundaries of our various allegiances. As we defend our actions at the water cooler we apply the force of our personal character and the direction of our personal convictions to the momentum and direction of the life of the group. Central to that drive is the deeply human yearning somehow to make a difference.

That is why it is important that the stories confront us with times of conflicting commitments. Dunbar is being held in the stockade at Fort Sedgewick. The major who is conducting the interrogation offers him a plea bargain. If Dunbar will become a scout and translator for the army, his conduct will be reevaluated. Dunbar is forced to choose, and in the end he chooses the Sioux. We have to make our choices, too, every day. The church is not the only group that competes for our attention and demands our loyalties, and our storytelling is crosshatched and riddled with borders that divide our internal lives and our social lives into hundreds of competing citizenships.

Among other things, I am a husband, a father, an American citizen, an Eagle Scout, a university professor, a minister, a writer, a licensed driver, and the Unofficial Grand Poobah of the International Fellowship of the Deep Belly Button. I have borrowing privileges at the local public library. I live in a small condominium in a working class neighborhood. All of these roles involve choices, and in the choices I make—and in the language I use to defend those choices—I discover clues about who I am. Part of who I am is the fact that my daughter Michal Beth is a graduate of Stanford University, my daughter Brynn plays harp, and my son Jonathan plays a mean blues guitar. On a daily basis, in a thousand ways, we choose where our primary loyalties lie.

## To Sum Up

Let us pause here and review where we have come with this chapter. In order for a social group to survive, it must have an effective way of establishing boundaries between insiders and outsiders, and for transitioning through these boundaries in either direction. It must have ways of differentiating roles, negotiating and enforcing lines of authority, establishing norms of behavior, and applying warrants and sanctions against group members who violate those norms. Joining a social group involves a series of steps by which we learn the rules about what is and is not acceptable, who the key players are, what words we can and cannot use, where the foundations of the old well are situated, who gives the order to "fire" when the enemy looms on the horizon, how the drumbeat should sound, where our tribe came from, and where we find wood for the winter.

Here I want to notice how absolutely central talk is in all of this. If we are to become members, real members, of any group, if we are ever going to get beyond official membership to become insiders, talk is the way we are going to do it. And if we're ever going to negotiate our way past the usher who guards the stage door, that negotiation is most likely to happen in the hallway or at the potluck table. In the end, it's the gossip that excludes outsiders that makes it possible for there to be insiders. It's the gossip that muscles and manipulates, and the gossip that throws the musclers and manipulators out of the ring. The gossip makes it possible for there to be a social hierarchy, and the gossip helps us reduce the hierarchy to size.

If talk is central to this process, the dynamic properties of language may require special attention if we are to understand the corresponding movements of power that are packaged up in the daily gossip. We turn to those properties in chapter 3.

The scene from *Dances with Wolves* with which this chapter opened depicts a decisive moment in the transformation of John Dunbar, but it is not an isolated moment. Instead, it culminates a long process of tiny encounters, transitions, and discoveries: His discovery of Stands with a Fist, alone on the prairie, lacerating herself with a knife in grief over the death of her first husband. A buffalo hunt. The discovery that whites have also been hunting the buffalo, but taking only the hides and leaving the carcasses to rot in the sun. The moment he is befriended by Kicking Bird, who eventually becomes his father-in-law. A battle with the Pawnee. An exchange of peace pipes. Each of these moments forms or transforms Lieutenant Dunbar in a small and imperceptible way. The transformation of John Dunbar is cumulative, and is so gradual that he himself is unaware of it. The scene in the stockade is only the flash point at which he realizes that he has indeed "gone Injun," and so we find him shouting in Sioux, "I have nothing to say to you. You are not worth talking to. I am Dances with Wolves."

So it is also with the community of faith. It is important that the church is made up of those who are called out; indeed, the very word "church" speaks to this reality. In Greek it is made up of two words, *ek*, which means "out of," and *kalein*, meaning "to call." But this truth is also a sociological one. The churches too have their special vocabularies—the languages by which they understand the meaning of that call and the way they respond to the claim it places upon them. We learn the lay of the land by talking with and about the others who live there; we take up our positions and stake out our own territories by telling and retelling our stories. We adopt the history of redemption as the clue to our own history. It is in the engagement with these things that we deepen or damage our Christian spirituality. If we do this well, by a hundred thousand tiny moments of spiritual formation, we come to be in practice what we are already by the grace of God—new creations in Christ.

In the church we also may experience a change of identity so deep that it entails a change of name. In early

Christianity it was not uncommon for converts to take conversion names as a way of declaring publicly that they were no longer quite the same. For Catholics, that practice lingers on in the custom of giving initiates new names as part of their formal initiation into the life of a monastery or convent. For Protestants the echoes are fainter, but still there, found mostly in our worship choruses:

*I will change your name.*
*You shall no longer be called*
*Wounded, outcast*
*Lonely or afraid*

*I will change your name,*
*Your new name shall be*
*Confidence, joyfulness*
*Overcoming one*
*Faithfulness, friend of God*
*One who seeks my face.*[5]

In a poignant moment at the end of the film, the Sioux chief Ten Bears speaks privately with Dances with Wolves after a tribe council meeting. Dances with Wolves has been dramatically rescued from the detail that was taking him in chains to Fort Hayes. Returned now to the Sioux village, he grows concerned that the army will send out a search party. He voices his concern in the council: The white soldiers will hunt a traitor long after they have given up on a mere enemy. If they find Dances with Wolves, they will also find the village. For everyone's sake—especially for the sake of the women and children—he will have to leave. Ten Bears dismisses the council so he can speak with Dances with Wolves alone: "The man the soldiers are looking for no longer exists," he says. "Now there is only a Sioux named Dances with Wolves."

CHAPTER THREE

# "I AIN'T LYIN'. I'M JUST IMPROVIN' THE TRUT'."

## A Short Course on Language

*"Just the facts, ma'am, just the facts."*
—Joe Friday, *Dragnet*

*"I ain't lyin'. I'm just improvin' the trut'."*
—Jack Kelly, *Newsies*

*On the most basic level, composing a personal story in our mind is the act of making order—or "sense"—out of a chaos of memories, thoughts, and emotions. Actually telling the story to others is the act of breaking out of an inscrutable silence into intelligible, meaningful language.*
—Jack Maquire

In the book, *Amusing Ourselves to Death*, Neil Postman makes an important and practical comment about the usefulness of different media for communicating different kinds of messages. Smoke signals, he says, are quite well suited for signaling danger over long distances, but are virtually useless for communicating philosophical ideas: "A Cherokee philosopher would run short of either wood or blankets before he reached his second axiom."[1] Postman's ultimate point is that the characteristics of electronic mass media are not well suited for the kinds of careful public discourse that can be better carried on in print. The point depends upon the assumption that the tools we use for a job both extend and limit the kinds of work we are able to do.

On a smaller scale I have found the same thing to be true about the differences between e-mail and regular mail, or between letters and telephone calls. My wife, Shaleen, and I spent the better part of our engagement on different coasts. She was in California, while I was away at seminary in Massachusetts. I remember how eagerly I looked forward to our weekly telephone conversations; they were always too short, were sometimes funny and affectionate, and were often frustrating (she reminds me of this as I write). The telephone calls were an important link that kept us connected. But it was the letters that brought out the best and most thoughtful side of our relationship. The letters were slower, and were sometimes hard to write. I labored over the prose. When Shaleen had something serious to discuss, she raised it in a letter. I genuinely believe that the depth of our present relationship twenty-three years later can be traced to the time and carefulness the letter writing forced upon us.

What Postman identifies, and what Shaleen and I experienced, is the hard-core reality that the nature of the medium changes the kinds of things that can be said or done. The instant exchange of information made possible by television and the Internet alters dramatically the landscape of public knowledge, as well as the politics of who has access to that information and how it will be used.

Lying behind this idea is a prior concern: Language itself is a medium of communication, and its specific properties determine the kinds of uses to which it can be put. A car is a tool that is well suited for moving us rapidly over the ground, but not for flight. A hoe is well suited for digging furrows in the ground, but not for hammering nails.

Language, too, is a tool that is well suited for some things, but not for others. In this chapter we examine that tool—what its basic properties are, and how those properties influence what we can and cannot do.

The mechanics of language can be sorted out into five basic parts, or features, each of which poses its own special problems and potentials for what we can say and what we hear.

**Language Is Selective**

*First, language is selective.* By this I mean that it cannot say everything, but must leave some things out. There's a physiological reason for this feature of language: The mind can only handle a certain amount of information per minute, rather like a river. Pump in more water than the river can handle, and it overflows its banks. Pump in more information than the mind can handle and the same thing happens—it washes out. I remember my fear that my college grades would be washed out by professors whose minds were able to process the outflow of information faster than I could process the inflow.

Consider the following short paragraph, read to a group of test subjects as the basis of a memory test:

> With hocked gems financing him, our hero bravely defied all scornful laughter that tried to prevent his scheme. Your eyes deceive you, he had said, an egg not a table correctly typifies this unexplored planet. Now three sisters sought proof, forging along sometimes through calm vastness, yet more often over turbulent peaks and valleys. Days became weeks as many doubters spread fearful rumors about the edge. At last, from nowhere, welcome winged creatures appeared, signifying momentous success.[2]

Another group of subjects was tested on the same paragraph, only this one with a title—"Columbus Discovers

America." To see what happened, now read the selection again.

The illustration above indicates something cognitive scientists call gap-filling. Because speakers must leave some things out, listeners must have some way of filling in the gaps in what is said. We can see this aspect of language at work any time there is a disruption in communication. Once Shaleen and I agreed to meet at the local high school to take the kids on a trip to the San Diego Zoo. Specifically, we agreed to meet where we usually pick up our daughter after school. What neither of us knew was that I usually picked her up by the gym, while Shaleen picked her up near the entrance of the school. We had filled in the gaps in different ways. My words run out about two hours and 100 miles later, so you will have to fill in the gaps for yourself about how she . . . and then I . . . and then both of us at once . . . and then my wife again . . . and then I . . . and then at last . . . friends again.[3]

**Language Is Linear**

*Second, language is linear.* By this I mean that it presents its information in a specific sequence. Nothing in the rules of logic requires that the sequence of the story be the same as the sequence of the actual events. Consider the following New England folktale:

> My Uncle Henry and my Aunt Mahitabel had an argument this past Christmastime. That's 'cause he didn't give his mother-in-law no Christmas present this year.
>
> 'Course, last year he gave the old woman a cemetery plot for Christmas.
>
> So this year, when Mahitabel started in on him, he said to her, "Now, Mahitabel. Why should I give your mother a Christmas gift this year when she never used the gift I gave her last year?"

This little tale starts with the current year, lapses back to the previous year, then returns to the current year.

Or consider the gap-filling in the following:

- John was on his way to school.
- He was terribly worried about the math lesson.
- He thought he might not be able to control the class again today.
- It was not a normal part of a janitor's job.[4]

In this series, the reader first construes one thing, then a different thing. As the "construals" meet and clash, they form a kind of linguistic pileup that ends with a tiny crash: "Aha! I've been had."

## Language Is Ambiguous

*Third, language is ambiguous.* This is a consequence of the fact that there are only a limited number of sounds in a language, sounds we combine and recombine into words. If a word could only have a single meaning, as new words are added to the language they would have to be longer and longer, like adding digits to license plates to account for the ever increasing number of cars. The way we deal with this is that we make single words do double duty; they mean one thing in one context, and a different thing in another context. One estimate has it that "the 500 most commonly used English words have an average of 28 dictionary meanings each."[5]

Jokes and other word plays depend heavily upon this feature of language:

"Know what happens when you don't pay your exorcist?"
"Nope. What?"
"You get repossessed."

Pundits have long enjoyed poking fun at double-sided newspaper headlines or advertising copy:

- Man wanted to work in dynamite factory. Must be willing to travel.
- Three-year-old teacher needed for preschool. Experience preferred.
- We do not tear your clothing with machinery. We do it carefully by hand.
- Tired of cleaning yourself? Let me do it.
- Auto repair service. Try us once. You'll never go anywhere again.
- Dog for sale. Eats anything and is fond of children.

### Language Has Aural Texture

*Fourth, language has aural texture*; it sounds a certain way on the ear. The texture of the language changes the way we respond. The same sentence means one thing shouted from the pulpit, and another thing whispered in the back pew. In the story, "Wiley and the Hairy Man," little Wiley has been sent by his mother on an errand to his grampa's house on the other side of the Yellow Belly Swamp.

> "This time I don't want you to go 'round the swamp the way you usually do," Mama tells Wiley. *When I tell this story, Mama has a low-pitched honey drawl.*
>
> "Mama, you trying to get rid of me?" Wiley asks. *His voice is high pitched and troubled.*
>
> "Land sakes, chile, why would you say a thing like that?" *Honey drawl.*
>
> "'Cuz you tole me that back in the swamp there lives a Hairy Man, and he wantsa eat me up." *Pitch is higher. Warbled with worry.*
>
> "You wuz little when I tole you that, Wiley. But you're bigger now. I think if you meet the Hairy Man, you could handle him sho'nuf. Now scat."

Two episodes later, deep in the swamp, Wiley really does meet the Hairy Man. Hairy Man grabs Wiley by the back of the neck. Turns him around.

> "Whachu doin' in here, boy?" *Hairy Man has a deep, gravelly voice. Barks at Wiley.* All Wiley can see is hair, and eyeballs, and . . . teeth.
>
> "Hello, Mr. Hairy Man. I knowed you was in here." *Wiley again. Cranes his neck to seem larger. The craning raises the pitch of his voice. Can't help that. His panic is masked by his diction. Wiley's trying to stay calm.*

The story goes on, of course. (In case you're wondering, Wiley makes it out alive. We return to his story in chapter 7.) The point of this brief clip is that the texture of the storyteller's voice has a marked effect on the listening process.

### Language Is Many-Sided

*Finally, language is many-sided.* By this I mean that it communicates on a number of levels—cognitive, emotional, personal, and social. We use language to encourage, enrage, comfort, convince, cajole, entertain, entrap, and any of a thousand other of the major things we do when we communicate. Consider the following speech, delivered by Mel Gibson in the role of William Wallace, just before the Battle of Stirling in the movie, *Braveheart*. The army of King Edward I—derisively called "Longshanks" in the movie—has lined up along one side of the battlefield. It is a truly impressive array—armored troops, cavalry, infantry, archers, and backup troops at the ready. The key factors here are the sheer size of the army, the skill of the archers, and the discipline of the troops. Wallace's Scottish rebels are arrayed on the other side—rag-tag, disheveled, disorganized. When they see Longshanks' army, they are ready to abandon the field. Like a thirteenth-century Winston Churchill, Wallace rises to the occasion with a speech that adds the needed ingredient—ferocity—and turns the tide of the battle.

> "I *am* William Wallace and I see a whole army of my countrymen, here in defiance of tyranny. You've come to fight as free men, and free men you are. What will you do without freedom? Will you fight?"
>
> "Against that?" someone objects. "No, we will run, and we will live."
>
> "Aye. Fight and you may die. Run and you'll live—at least for a while. And dying in your beds, many years from now, would you be willing to trade all the days from this one to that, for one chance—just one chance—to come back here and tell our enemies that they may take our lives, but they will never take our freedom!"

By the time Mel Gibson finished delivering this speech I wanted to get up and join the fray! The graphic violence moments later changed my mind.

**To Sum Up Thus Far**

In essence, then, there are five basic features of language.[6]

- *Language is selective.* It cannot present every detail of the story line without becoming unmanageable.
- *Language is linear.* It presents its information in a specific sequence, one word after another.
- *Language is inherently ambiguous.* Because words must do double duty, language is always potentially ambiguous.
- *Language has aural texture.* It sounds a certain way on the ear.
- *Language is many-sided.* It carries meaning on a variety of levels—emotional, cognitive, social, and personal.

Each of these features of language poses its own distinctive problems for its users. For example, the fact that language is linear means that a speaker will have difficulty presenting events that happened at the same time. What he or she will do is present first one, then the other, with a kind of "meanwhile, back at the ranch" explanatory aside. Whereas in real time these things happened simultaneously, in the *story* time, they happen in *sequence*.

Problems such as these are difficult to avoid but, as we shall see in chapter 4, are quite easy to exploit. In order to speak at all I must overcome the difficulties on the production side, and in order to understand what is said my listener has to overcome them from the reception side.

## All Storytelling Is Interpretation

The important thing to note here is that we cannot tell a story about anything at all without interpreting the event in some way. The basic features of language create insurmountable differences between an event and any story we might tell about the event. Let's represent that difference with a diagram. In the following, let the series of blocks represent some event that has happened, as it happened, in its entirety. Imagine that everything is in the mix—what everyone was wearing, the color of the sky, the number of clouds, the amount of energy everyone had, their ages, their conscious and unconscious motivations. Everything.

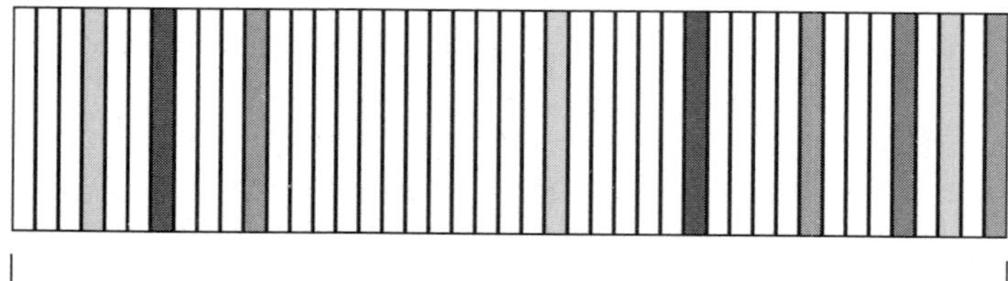

*EVENT*

If I want to talk about the event in any way at all, I have to leave some things out. This is because language is inherently selective. The fact that I have to leave some things out forces me to make decisions about what's important and what's not.

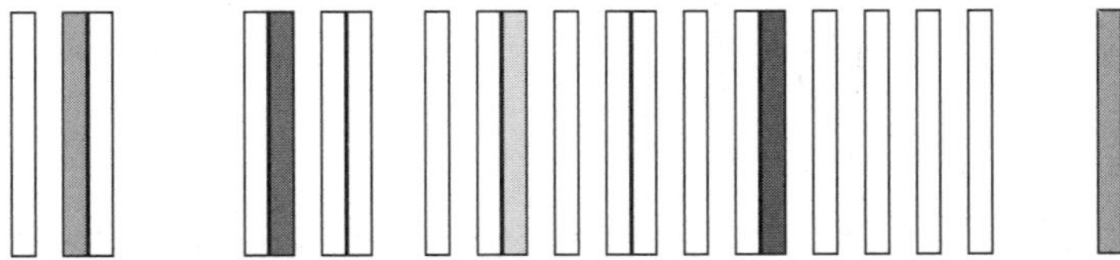

I will also condense some parts of the story. The resulting story is almost always shorter than the original event.

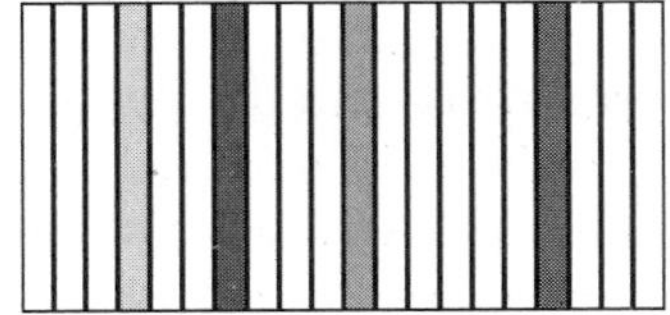

But I also may choose to elaborate some parts in great detail, to give them what I take to be their proper weight.

Because language is linear, I must decide the sequence in which I am going to tell my story. I do not have to tell the story in the same sequence as the one in which it actually happened.

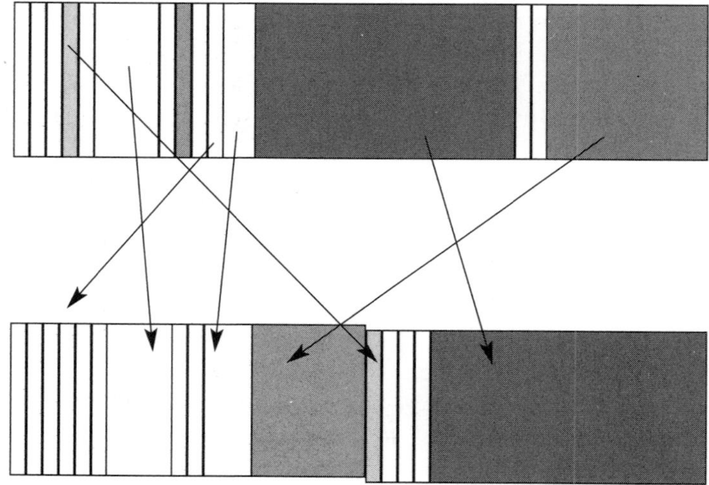

I must also decide what words to use, and what I am going to imply by my choice of words. This is related to the ambiguity and the polyvalence of language. I will also need to add explanations and other asides to help my listeners find their way around in the story.

If we compare the story with the original event we can see that they are quite different, and are related to each other in complex ways.

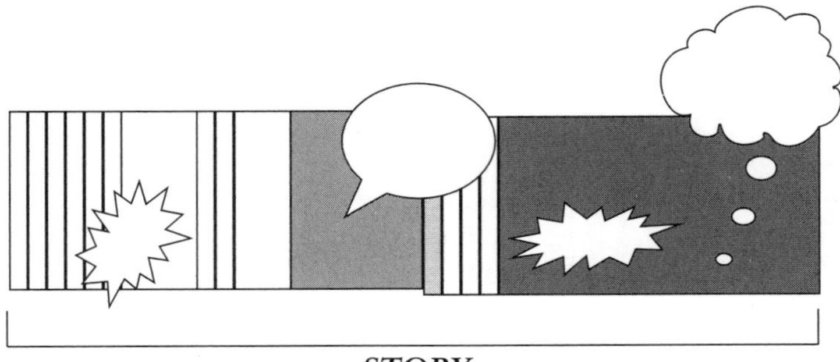

*STORY*

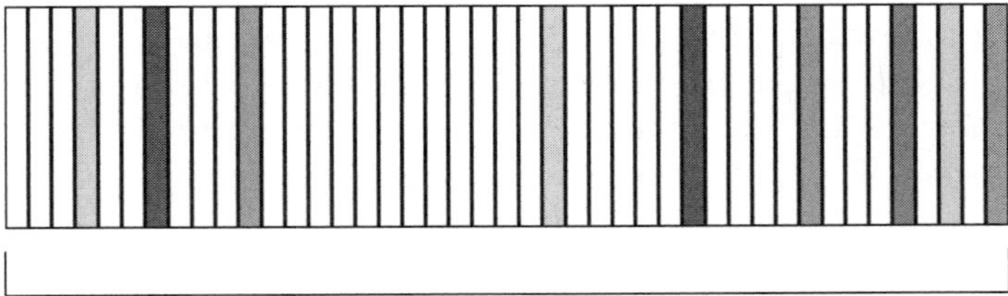

*EVENT*

The relationship between an event and the story about the event is never a simple one, but always involves a series of strategic interpretive moves. This is true whether the story is part of a news report, something from the opinion section of the newspaper, an illustration in a sermon, a full-length novel, or simple table conversation such as gossip.

In an eloquent description of these retrospective rememberings, Stephen Crites reflects on the basic narrative quality of experience itself:

> Images do not exist in memory as atomic units, like photographs in an album, but as transient episodes in an image-stream, cinematic, which I must suspend and from which I must abstract in order to isolate a particular image. The most direct and obvious way of recollecting it is by telling a

> story, though the story is never simply the tedious and unilluminating recital of the chronicle of memory itself. And, of course, I can manipulate the image-stream in other ways. I can abstract general features and formal elements of it for purposes of theory, or suspend it in order to draw a picture, or splice episodes from it in a way that gives them new significance. I can contemplate a whole segment of the image stream in a single glance of inner vision, then fragment it so that its elements are left twinkling in isolation like stars.[7]

On the TV cop show *Dragnet* Detective Joe Friday used to punctuate his interviews with witnesses by asking for "Just the facts, ma'am, just the facts." But somebody has to decide which facts are important and which are not. There's no way to get around the fact that Friday's witnesses were interpreting what they saw even as they reported "just the facts." The bottom line is this: *We cannot gossip at all without* ***interpreting*** *the events we're gossiping about.* All storytelling is interpretation.

## All Interpretation Is Storytelling

But the opposite is also true: It's this distance between an event and the story about the event that makes it possible for us to come to understanding in the first place. Something happens, and as we talk about it we assign relative significances to the various parts, decide what's irrelevant and can be dropped, decide what's important and should be elaborated, decide what language to use, decide what to imply with our language, decide what context to talk about it at all, decide that other contexts are iffy or inappropriate altogether, and decide who we can tell and whom we cannot. In all of this deciding we come to terms with the event and make it our own, just as my daughter Brynn did in her story about the Mexican girl Marisa who broke her candy into pieces for her brothers.

Indeed, if there is a single central reason why we talk at

all it is this. This is the reason we cannot hope to be the church without the talk. It is only because of the daily conversations, the telephone calls, the reports to the congregation, the chatting in the parking lot that we can come to understand at all what has happened to us. Perhaps we will do this bluntly, or even brutally. Sometimes we become our own spin doctors, slanting the story to make a quick sale with our audience, as the character Jack Kelly does in the movie, *Newsies*. "I ain't lyin'," he says. "I'm jus' improvin' the trut'." But we can also tell our stories with grace and color. One interpreter of the inner life, psychologist Thomas Moore, describes this process as "the art of reading our experiences into poetry."[8]

Perhaps that process is at the root of our deep hunger for stories and storytelling. In a wonderful essay on *The Healing Power of Stories,* Daniel Taylor points out that there are sources of stories everywhere—family, education, religion, and popular media. "Deprive children of stories," he says, quoting Alisdair MacIntyre, "and you leave them unscripted, anxious stutterers in their actions as in their words."[9] Taylor continues:

> The story quality of our own lives is apparent in many common features of everyday life: our love of gossip, nostalgia, and reminiscence; our desire to explain ourselves and our actions—to be understood; our near-obsession with the self, self-actualization, self-improvement; our penchant for analyzing in exhausting detail our relationships with others; our habit of dreaming and daydreaming; the desire to do things that are exciting, interesting, unusual; our limited but genuine love of surprise and the unexpected; our fundamental desire to feel that we are moral; our agonizing over choices; our concern for what will happen next, and for the future and how things will "turn out"; and, perhaps most powerful of all, our fundamental mental desire that our lives mean something.[10]

Taylor could not have given us a more fitting description of the underlying drives that spark our quest for spirituality. Not fear of dying, but fear of never having lived.

## Without a Storyteller There Is No Story

The fact that a story is the result of hundreds of interpretive decisions also signals an important factor in the movement from an event to the daily gossip about the event: Between the event and the gossip there are always storytellers, who cannot help but imprint their own points of view on the story as they tell. In essence, the storyteller acts the part of a living filter, adapting the details of the story to the needs of the moment, omitting—or perhaps elaborating!—what is taboo or distasteful, arranging sequences with an eye toward creating just the right impression, *implying* what perhaps should not be said outright.

The presence of the storyteller also raises the critical question that will occupy our attention in chapter 4: What governs this process of interpretation? What drives and controls the movement from *event* to the *gossip about the event?* The storyteller drives the story, but what drives the storyteller?

CHAPTER FOUR

# THE SWORD OF OUR MOUTH

## Cutting Remarks That Cut People Out

*If any think they are religious,*
*and do not bridle their tongues*
*but deceive their hearts,*
*their religion is worthless.*
—James 1:26

For several months in 1993 and 1994, John served as interim "minister of the pulpit" for a small congregation near his home as it searched for a full-time pastor. Another intern provided pastoral care, while the members of the congregation themselves managed the practical affairs of the church. It was a satisfying time, as John learned to face the special challenges of preparing a fresh sermon every week.

In the spring of 1994, when the Pastoral Nominating Committee submitted a name to the congregation for consideration, John found that he had himself been nominated. It was an honor and a fresh challenge that he accepted with reluctance only because he was afraid that the full-time commitment would interfere with his schooling. The vote of the congregation was not unanimous, but showed a healthy margin of support. John's vocation as a preacher and pastor was launched the way many are launched, a little at a time.

Within a week all chaos broke loose. The rumor mill began chewing John up. According to the rumors, his sermons were no longer clear or biblical. He was overstepping his bounds as a church leader, making unwise decisions about church programs and finances, and ignoring his pastoral responsibilities to the sick and troubled. There were attacks against his character. As he left the church one Sunday morning, one of the deacons confronted him in the parking lot. "Just remember," said the deacon, "we're watching every move you make!" That was when John came to me for advice.

What happened here? This is another way of posing the question with which chapter 3 closed. What drives the storyteller to shape the story in one direction, rather than another? What governs the flow of the gossip? Here we will explore five contributing factors.

## We Gossip to Be Part of the Conversation

The first has to do with one of the rules of basic etiquette: We want to make sure that our two cents worth connects with the thread of the conversation. Indeed, responding in kind is one of the ways we show our conversation partners that we're actually listening to them. As we listen to the table talk, we search our memories for similar stories that we can add to the mix. We also listen for cues we can use to segue into our own contribution—"I know what you mean, she did something like that to me once." That way we can be contributors to the talk, rather than merely listeners. It's the social equivalent of horse-trading. Trade a tidbit for a different tidbit; no money changes hands but everybody walks away feeling a little richer. The result of this tendency is that in the horse-trading world of gossip, we tend to gather similar and related stories into the same corral.

Sometimes this can be quite positive and enlightening. Sometimes it's harmless fun. One of my seminary professors was noted for two things: his brilliance (he was a prolific scholar who wrote masterful studies on a wide variety of topics) and his absent-mindedness. So he had an intriguing persona. I can remember sitting with the other students over lunch, swapping absent-minded Professor Luftus stories.

Student One:

"Once I came upon Professor Luftus standing by his car, staring at the keys in his hand.

'Are you all right, Professor Luftus?' I asked.

'Not really,' Professor Luftus replied. 'I can't remember whether I'm getting out of my car and going to my office, or getting in my car and going home.' "

Student Two chimes in:

"Once Professor Luftus' wife dropped him off for class while she went to run some errands. She came back early to get him, and parked the car in front of Kerr Hall. She went in the front door to find him, while he came out the side door to meet her. When he saw the car, he thought he had brought it, so he got in it and drove home. Had to come back and get her."

Student Three:

"Did you know that he used to wear a note pinned to his lapel that said, 'DO NOT GIVE ME A RIDE HOME, I HAVE THE CAR TODAY.' "

Student One again:

"Once Professor Luftus and his wife woke up in the night because their baby was coughing. The baby had a high temperature, so they called the doctor, who told them that it sounded serious and he would meet them at the emergency room. They rushed out, jumped in the car, and drove helter-skelter for the hospital, only to discover when they were pulling into the hospital parking lot that they had forgotten to bring the baby!"

So it goes. The collection of Professor Luftus stories is quite large, and no doubt is growing even as I write. Sometimes a single central thread ties the stories together, but sometimes they change direction. "A lot of professors are like that. Have you heard what A. D. Nock did once?" There's a hiccup in the conversation, a change of direction, and we're discussing something that's different but not different.

The thread of the conversation also gives hints to the listeners about how they're supposed to hear the stories. I know that when I hear absent-minded Professor Luftus stories I should laugh and pitch in one of my own:

> "Once"—this is true, by the way—"I saw Professor Luftus standing by the photocopy machine, waiting for some copies that were feeding into the bin. He had a kind of distracted look on his face.
>
> 'Are you all right, Professor Luftus?' I asked.
>
> 'They're not true, you know,' he said.
>
> 'What aren't true?'
>
> 'All those absent-minded professor stories everyone is telling you.'
>
> 'Oh, those. All right,' I said. 'I'll take your word on that.'
>
> 'Good,' he said.
>
> And then he walked away and left his photocopies in the bin."

Sometimes the collections are less charitable. This is part of what happened with John. As parishioners became aware of the rumors they searched their memories for other stories that matched the thread of the rumors they were hearing, adding them into the mix. What began as a little snowball throwing ended up as an avalanche.

## We Gossip to Be Interesting

The second factor that governs the movement from an event to the gossip about the event is that we want our contribution to be *interesting*. But this is a relative term. It is a tragedy of modern life that what is interesting to a university professor is not what is interesting to a university freshman. What is interesting to an American may be an incredible bore to a Greek or Chinese. In general, we can solve this little problem with a rule of thumb: *So far as gossip is concerned, something is interesting to the extent that it violates cultural norms.* The infraction can range from personal eccentricities (Professor Luftus again) to breaches of etiquette ("I can't believe they actually served *ham* at Easter. Everyone knows the *proper* food for Easter is lamb!"), to wild-eyed violations of social taboo, to deliberate and knowing violations of international law.

On the other hand, we tend *not* to find the norm itself very interesting, and we seldom talk about it except in passing. The following dialogue takes place on board ship, where the first mate has been found drunk.

> The captain, being a strong-minded and upright man, has made an entry in the log: *"The first mate was drunk last night."*
>
> "Please, sir," says the first mate. "There's no rule against drinking, and I was off duty. No harm done. Won't you please strike the record from the log?"
>
> "Not on your life!" roars the captain. "I'm a religious man, and no true word has ever been struck from my ship's log! Now off with you!"
>
> The next night when the captain comes on duty, he finds the following entry, neatly scribed in the first mate's hand: *"The captain was sober last night."*

In this context it is important to remember that culture is not a monolith at all, but a plurality of diverse and competing subcultures. What is normal for one group may be frightening or alienating for another. Recently I was in Romania, working with a group of Pentecostal pastors. The director of our trip was a highly skilled and articulate woman named

Lydia Sarandan from one of our local Presbyterian churches. Lydia has a Doctor of Ministry degree, and is a highly respected leader, not only in her own congregation, but throughout our local presbytery. She had very much to say, and everything she had to say the Romanians needed to hear, but the conversation was almost derailed by the fact that what was normal for *us*—that our women wear jewelry and makeup—was a matter of issue for *them*. The talk about the jewelry nearly drowned out the talk about ministry—on both sides of the cultural divide.

So it goes. Denominational groups. National allegiances. Community service organizations. Families. Each group that claims our loyalties also in some way tests those loyalties by looking for willingness to live within norms. When those norms are violated, they raise not only eyebrows, but also danger signals and warning flags. People perk up their ears and begin asking questions. This process fuels the fires of gossip because it makes everything so terribly *interesting*.

### We Gossip to Manage Power

This leads us to the third factor that drives the movement from *event* to *gossip*—the management of power. In essence, the movement from event to story is an opportunity for social maneuvering. In chapter 3 we discussed five basic features of language. On one level, each of these is a problem that speakers and listeners must overcome in order for meaningful communication to take place, but on another level, it is precisely these features of language that make it such a useful tool for making our way in the world. That's because listeners must deal with these things in predictable ways, and that predictability makes it possible for speakers to manipulate what listeners are likely to do.

For example, because language is linear, we can say something up front to provide a context in which the listener will understand what comes later in a certain way. When I was a boy, I often found myself preparing for difficult conversations with my father. When my father had *that tone* in his voice I knew I was in trouble. I can still remember the chill that would run down my spine as I went to face the music. More to the point, I remember strategizing my defense for whatever it was I had done. I knew that the opening steps in the defense were the most important ones, and so I would start with an analysis of the context, always hoping to show that it was somehow *necessary* that I had done what I had done. I also knew to pack the word "sir" in there somewhere, and that I should hold back my best excuses for the final appeal. I was never very good at this simple form of childhood rhetoric, as the bruises on my adult psyche have shown.

Sometimes we use the linearity of language to entrap our listeners into a particular point of view. Several years ago my son played on a soccer team in which both the coach and the assistant coach used quite abusive language. I won't repeat that language here, but I'll ask you to trust me that it was very strong. I called the coach.

"Coach, my son tells me that the assistant coach has been using pretty strong language with the boys. Do you know anything about that?"

"Some of the other parents said that he does."

"Do you understand that that's really unacceptable to us?"

"Yes. I hear your concern, but he's usually on the far end of the field, so I haven't actually heard him use that language myself."

"Sure, coach, but you're the head coach, and you're responsible for what the assistant coach does. Aren't you?"

"I suppose I am."

"Do I have your word that you'll solve this problem with the assistant coach, then?"

"I'll talk to him."

"And you agree with me that that sort of language is completely unacceptable with the boys?"

"Absolutely!"

"Then in that case, coach, we may have another problem. My son reports to me that you use the same language."

We never had another problem with either coach, and at least a part of the reason was that I had taken the time to strategize the sequence in which the conversation would unfold. Not only did I strategize the sequence of the original conversation, I also strategized where I would place it in this book. When I reported this conversation back to my son, he learned—quite effectively but secondhand—how to manage a difficult situation involving language and the play of power. In those contexts, it served a completely different purpose than it did that day on the telephone.

**We Gossip to Reduce Our Sense of Anxiety**

My conversation with the coach illustrates a very different way in which we use language to manage power—"verbal dueling." Most verbal duels involve trivial matters of position and status in the conversation itself. Sometimes the stakes are much higher, as in the following conversation between the African-American psychiatrist Alvin Pouissant, and a white police officer in Jackson, Mississippi. Exactly fifteen words are exchanged between them.

The police officer speaks first:

"What's your name, boy?"
"Dr. Pouissant. I'm a physician."
"What's your first name, boy?"
"Alvin."

Here is clearly a duel with a winner and a loser. For Pouissant it is a moment of danger; the police officer carries a shield, and he fights with a broadax and cudgel. Pouissant's only weapon is his wit—the sword of his mouth. The police officer's opening swing is driven in with greater force by the edge he will have placed on his voice: "*What's your name, boy?*" His eyes are focused squarely on Pouissant's face.

Pouissant sidesteps the blow and returns a parry, phrasing his thrust very carefully to assert the status claim of his education without pushing the police officer to the limits. "*Dr. Pouissant.*" The parry is followed by a short riposte—"*I'm a physician*"—given to drive home the point, though surely given quietly. The police officer sweeps aside the parry and riposte by dismissing Pouissant's title as irrelevant, and by discounting his surname. He ups the ante by sharpening the edge on his voice, and then takes a swing: "*What's your first name, boy?*" It is too much; Pouissant staggers under the force of the blow. He turns his eyes down and drops his voice away. In reporting this exchange later, Pouissant tells us that his final response, "*Alvin,*" was given with "profoundest humiliation."[1]

Let's imagine that there were others present at this scene, say, Pouissant's wife and fourteen-year-old son in the car, and two or three "good ol' boys" watching from the curb. (I have no idea whether or not Dr. Pouissant is even married, much less a father, but work with me here.) A duel that is fought in the presence of an audience takes on a different aspect. The gallery not only observes the duel, but in a real and meaningful way it participates in it. The presence of onlookers raises the stakes by intensifying all of the status issues involved. This makes a significant difference in the thrust and parry, and the duelers play not only to win, but also to save face or to score a hit with the gallery.

Here's where gossip enters the picture. We use gossip as a means of extending the gallery, in essence fighting the duel over again, only this time on our own turf. We pick the context with an eye toward securing the home court advantage. In this way we can reduce our sense of threat—the fourth factor that influences the movement from event to gossip. Gerhard Lohfink gives us another example of a verbal duel, only this one fought on different turf, long after the actual battle sounds have died away:

> Have you ever observed the way such battles are reported? The reporter comes off as a model of tranquillity and patience, the opponent is a howling savage. It goes like this: "I said, 'Mr. Winkler,' I said—'that new filing system won't work!'" (This is said in the quietest tone in the world, mild, detached, wise.) "He said, 'I beg your pardon!' he said—'I designed this system personally.'" (This is said quickly, violently, angrily.) Now the cool head again: "I said, very quietly, I said, 'Mr. Winkler,' I said, 'we can't file letters like that or else the C mail will get mixed up with the D mail!' "
>
> The description of the dispute at work continues; it reaches its climax and breaks off with the question, "Can you beat that?"[2]

Even without a blow-by-blow analysis it is clear that the speaker is carrying on a battle. What he is fighting for is reassurance, or, to state the same thing on the obverse, the reduction of anxiety, which his listener's sympathetic head nods and murmurs offer. Winkler, depending upon his degree of self-assurance, may well be rehearsing this scene from a different vantage point as he tosses back a tall one at the local Executives Club.

### We Gossip So We Don't Feel Alone

What the unnamed speaker is doing here is a specialized form of verbal dueling called *triangling*. He lowers his anxieties about Winkler by bringing in a third party. After all, Winkler is his boss, and wisdom cautions against going in for a kill. Notice that Mr. Winkler, the boss, has been stylized and flattened, and while his motives are not described, the listener is asked to construct them in a narrow, black-and-white way. The closing question—"*Can you beat that?*"—asks the listener for reassurance that this is indeed the legitimate interpretation of what happened. Every aspect of the exchange is calculated to bring the listener to this response.

Imagine a triangle in which the angles and length of the sides can change, but the total length of the sides must remain the same. As the triangle develops it draws the speaker and listener closer together, but it can only do so by pushing the person being talked about farther away, like this exchange, in which the speaker triangles his friend against his boss.

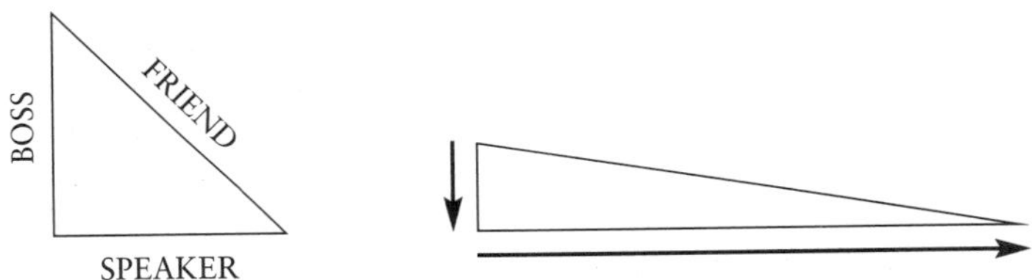


How does the listener respond to this closing question? One way is to defend Winkler, in which case the conversation will either heat up or shut down. Another, less volatile way, is for the listener to agree, and toss in a story of his or her own. We have seen already that one of the driving factors in the movement from event to story is the need to fit our contributions into the thread of the conversation. Witness the absent-minded Professor Luftus stories. The same sorts of conversational dynamics can work when I'm triangling or being triangled. The resulting accumulation of stories is called injustice collecting. Partners in the conversation can string together a long series of injustices to make a collection, in which each one reinforces and legitimizes the others.

It's important to notice that the effect of this process is both selective and cumulative. In real time and real space the injustices may have been spread out over a long period of time. They could even have been interspersed with genuine expressions of care and concern, or with attempts on the part of the person being talked about to bring reconciliation and healing. But, since those more positive elements get left out of the injustice collection, the overall effect, while perfectly accurate, can be quite misleading. Characters are flattened, their motives are questioned, and in the end they turn out to be tramps and thieves. This is another part of what happened to John. His attempts to resolve the difficulties in the church were swept under the rug and forgotten. He found himself being lynched in the court of public opinion without a fair trial.

There are payoffs in these exchanges. The person doing the triangling gets reassurance that he or she is right after all, while the person being triangled gets the reassurance of being a trusted confidant, an insider. But there are costs as well. Injustice collecting can start out as a genuine effort to make everything come out right. The cry for justice is an ever-present part of the human experience, and we are better for it, but it can also turn out to be a bargain with the devil.

**To Sum Up Thus Far**

What we have seen in this chapter and chapter 3 is that we can't tell any story at all without interpreting the events we're talking about. This goes for every kind of story—news report, novel, sermon illustration, gossip, everything. Whenever we tell a story we make—sometimes subconsciously—a whole series of interpretive decisions, about what to include, what to leave out, what language to use, what to imply, and what to state outright.

Thus far we have seen that the movement from the *event* to gossip *about* the event is driven by five engines:

- The need to connect to the thread of the conversation
- The need to be interesting
- The need to manage power
- The need to reduce anxiety
- Our deep hunger not to feel alone

What these five things have in common is our need to be included and taken seriously in the social groups and communities in which we find ourselves. We also want to be liked, to be respected, and to be *wanted*, as Sabini and Silber point out:

> Typically, when we gossip, we tell a story we claim to know to someone who doesn't. This gives us a certain latitude with the material to remove conflicting details, heighten the moral point, improve our role in the matter, or at least remove jarring intimations about our own motives and faux pas. We are likely to come off well.[3]

**We Want to Be Believed**

Our deep desire to "come off well" implies a sixth factor that governs the movement from *event* to *story*, which serves as a kind of brake on our freedom of movement: We want our contribution to the conversation to be believed. Even the most ordinary and innocent of conversations reflect our yearning to be believed, to be taken seriously. The need to be believed is naturally shaped by the ways the other members of our group tend to interpret reality. Those interpretive habits—which I call the hermeneutic of everyday life—control what we can and cannot say within our group.

In a sense, the hermeneutic of everyday life governs the overall content of our gossip in the same way that the rules of grammar govern the structure of our sentences. We don't usually think about grammar because it does its work subconsciously, but the fact that we don't think about it doesn't mean it isn't there or that it's unimportant. If I use improper grammar in my classroom, very soon I will be faced with difficult conversations with the college dean. In the same way, if we tend to interpret our experiences in ways that violate the hermeneutic for our group, we will mark ourselves as outsiders.

Suppose I have been fired from my job. Depending upon the ways my friends talk about such things, I can follow any number of strategies to tell them what happened but keep my dignity intact. I might tell them my boss is incompetent, and then give evidence to support that claim. I might assert that I did not like the work, and that I'm better off without that stupid job anyway. I might tell them that the loss of the job was an attack of the devil, who wants to keep me from sharing my faith with customers. Or, I may claim that it was the will of God, who is sovereignly moving me to a place where I can be of greater use in the kingdom.

My pastor friend John reported to me that when he discussed the problem of the rumors with the members of the Elder Board he got mixed reactions. One elder told him over lunch that the trouble in the church was clearly the work of God, who was "refining the church by weeding out the troublemakers who were leaving in dismay." Another told him with equal conviction that the trouble was the work of the devil, who was "scattering the sheep by attacking the shepherd." As John reported to me these two explanations, I wondered how either would fly if they had been offered at a business meeting in the companies where these two men worked. As they explained what was going on, they conformed their talk to the vocabulary, language habits, and points of view they thought would be appropriate and compelling in the social context of the church.

It seems clear that the hermeneutic of everyday life is one of the major boundary markers between members of differing social groups. The very business of joining a group involves adopting the rules that govern the group's talk. Despite their common personal history, Dances with Wolves is a very different person from John J. Dunbar. The fact that he sees the world differently is reflected not only in his shift from English to Sioux, but also in the things he chooses to say and not say with his new language. We all make these adjustments to our language. If we don't, our telling won't appear credible to our hearers, and sooner or later they'll stop asking our opinion, we'll be dropped from the dinner group, or we'll be overlooked for that big promotion. As we saw in chapter 2, when we join a social group, one of the ways we pay our admission price is to learn to talk about reality the same way as the other members of the group.

We learn to make these little concessions to social custom very early on. Consider the case of children on the playground, sharing their accounts of how they won the handball match. As each one gives his or her report of what happened, a delicate negotiation takes place. Each child watches the others for their reactions to the talk. If the telling elicits negative responses, the teller will subtly reshape the story until it proves more credible in the hearing of the group. This little game of challenge and response that engages the energies of children on the playground is actually played out in every kind of social relationship, on every level. Language is a game with winners and losers, and when we play we spar for our place in the social hierarchy of the group. If our stories aren't believable, the other players eventually take their ball and go home.

### To Sum Up

Thus, we have two basic movements—our motives for talking drive the gossip forward, and our desire to be believed reins us in and limits what we can and cannot say. We can stretch the limits of truth only so far, but stretch the truth we do sometimes, and our motives for gossiping face us with critical moral dilemmas. Perhaps nowhere is this more evident than when we feel ourselves to be under threat. The perception of threat squeezes the color out of the issues and turns everything black and white, and the greater the sense of threat, the more this is likely to happen. It's hard to gossip sympathetically about someone whose actions have made us feel vulnerable or exposed. Indeed, the degree of injustice collecting in a community's gossip is a telling indicator of its larger sense of anxiety! All of this yields a kind of guideline: *The degree of threat present appears to have an effect on the ways we interpret the events we're gossiping about. The greater our need to reduce our anxiety, the more distrustful and judgmental our gossip will likely be.*

This, I believe, is finally behind what happened to John and his congregation. The shift of status from interim to full-time pastor upset the existing power structure of the church. This was a church that had cared for its own physical and spiritual needs for a long time and suddenly it had to adjust to a new presence, or rather, to an old presence that had a new role to play. As John assumed his responsibilities as pastor, he unwittingly stepped on toes. The result was a heightened sense of collective anxiety, which turned the gossip ugly.

In the end he found out that the toes he had stepped on belonged to a single person—the organist. The rumors were the organist's way of paying back. As the organist worked her telephones, she exploited all of the basic properties of language. She left things out. She attended to sequence. She made good use of double meanings to suggest what she dared not say outright. She added interpretive asides. She began by choosing her triangling partners very carefully, harvesting ideas from their feedback. She selected out deviations from the norm to emphasize. Where there were none, she invented them. She played down John's history with the church, and played up the elements that had changed. She used the language of theology and pastoral care to attack his competence. She attacked his character and his motives.

She wanted him *gone*.

If the telling of stories is driven by motives, the listening is also driven by motives. We turn to the question of listening in chapter 5.

CHAPTER FIVE

# GOOD NEWS AND BAD NEWS

## Lori, David, and the Princess Who Lived in a Prison

*O Jesus, Son of God, who was silent before Pilate.*
*Do not let us wag our tongues without thinking of*
*what we are to say, and how we are to say it.*
—Gaelic Prayer

It was a hot afternoon in New Testament Survey. We had effectively covered the material for the day, and the students in the class had finished off their notes, closed their notebooks, and packed everything away in their backpacks. Someone asked for a story, so I told them the story of "The Princess Who Lived in a Prison."[1]

The story involves a young princess who had used mud to mortise sticks into the windows of her playhouse to form bars. Then she began spending her time in the "safety" of this odd little place. Her friends stopped playing with her because they found this behavior peculiar and a little frightening. Every day she locked herself away, often sitting on her cot for long hours at a time. The king was beside himself with worry, but did not know what to do. Eventually a traveler appeared, befriending the girl by talking to her through the bars of the window. In time he earned her trust. We pick up the story after weeks of conversation. The princess has ventured out with the stranger, and in time has grown as comfortable outside the prison as she was inside.

One day, as they were returning from a long walk in the forest, they stopped on the edge of the meadow to look at the prison from a distance.

"It doesn't suit you anymore," he said. "Why don't you let me tear it down?"

"No," she said. "I built it with my own two hands. I will tear it down myself."

And so the traveler went and sat on a log and watched, while the princess carefully dismantled the prison and gently laid its pieces out into the meadow where the rain could wash them back into the earth from which they had come. Then she went over and stood beside him.

"There," she said. "It's gone. I don't live there anymore."

I finished the story and dismissed the class. As we left I heard little clusters of students wondering out loud what the story must mean.

The next day I was working in my office when I was interrupted by a terrible, angry pounding on my office door. I opened the door and there stood one of my students—I'll call her Lori. Beside her stood her husband, whom I'll call David. He was red-faced and angry and he nearly forced his way past me into my office:

"Why did you expose my wife to public ridicule yesterday in class?"

"Come in, David. Hello, Lori. Why not have a seat?"

"Why did you expose my wife to public ridicule?"

"What are we talking about here?"

"That story about the princess and the prison."

"What about it?"

"Lori was humiliated by that story. You told the whole class that she had not yet finished her therapy! How could you do that to her? Didn't you know she was fragile? Didn't you even *care*?" David is a large man, and it was clear that he intended to punch me out.

"Let me ask you something, David," I said. "What makes you think that *I* knew that Lori was in therapy?"

He softened a little. "Well, maybe you didn't."

"Did I use Lori's name in the story?"

He softened a little more, "Lori, did he?"

Lori: "No."

Me again: "Lori, you sit in the back row. Did any of the other students turn to look at you as I told the story?"

Lori: "No, I don't think so."

Me: "Did anyone say anything to you about the story after class?"

Lori: "Well, no."

Me: "David, do you still think that I exposed Lori to public ridicule?"

In this chapter, we examine what happened with Lori. What transpired between my *telling* of the story and Lori's *hearing* of it? What movements of the mind or heart had Lori gone through that would make her feel exposed in that way?

## Problems for Listeners Are Opportunities for Tellers

In chapter 3 I sketched briefly a series of five basic characteristics of language. Language is *selective*, it's *linear*, it's *ambiguous*, it has *aural texture*, and it's *many-sided*. Each of these features of language poses its own unique problems for communication. There is an important implication here for the ways in which we talk about life. Each of those problems creates its own unique opportunities for strategizing the way we present the material of the story. We discussed these in chapter 4. The fact that language is selective means that we can leave certain things out; the fact that it's linear means that we can present information early to prepare our listeners to hear later information in a particular way, or hold back critical information to create suspense or surprise.

What makes all this strategizing actually work is found

on the other side of the interpretive process, in the things readers and listeners must do to *decode* the story. The critical point here is that the decoding is a patterned process, rather than a random one. The patterns involve a series of strategic interpretive moves demanded by the features of language. For example, because language is linear, we have to create a sense of the whole, but we have to work with one part at a time. We do this by balancing two mental activities. First, we guess where the speaker is going, then we correct our guess when more adequate information arrives. One could say that this movement is dialectical: it oscillates back and forth.

As we listen to language unfold one word after another, we have a similar movement between *projection* and *retrospection*. First we project what is coming; then we retrospect and correct any misperceptions we may have formed in our projection. It is this oscillating movement that gives jokes their ability to startle us:

> When I found a skull in the woods, the first thing I did was call the police. But then I got curious about it. I picked it up, and started wondering who this person was, and why he had deer horns.[2]

The same holds true for the other features of language. Because language is selective, when we listen we have to find ways of filling in the gaps in what is said. Because language is both ambiguous and polyvalent, we have to have ways of deciding which of the possible meanings are actually intended, and which are not. Because language has aural texture, we have to have ways of taking the effects of the sound into account and responding appropriately.

As we saw in chapter 4, this gives the speaker a certain leverage. By managing the sequence and wording of our gossip, we can also manage the responses and reactions our listeners are likely to have. We can focus on juicy parts about the other fellow, but omit entirely the parts that make us look bad. We can question peoples' motives. We can say something early on to shape what our listeners think of later parts of the story. We can whisper our lines so our listeners will know that they're being let in on some special tidbit that isn't part of the common knowledge. We can do this because we know that our listeners play the corresponding role of filling in gaps, unscrambling sequences, disambiguating, and responding to clues of texture and so forth. It's a bit like a dance, with the speaker leading and the listener following. When it goes well, neither one is consciously aware of what's happening, but when it goes badly we hobble away with bruises on our toes and (maybe worse) our pride.

Of all of these things that our listeners are doing, by far the most important has to do with the way they fill in the gaps of the story.[3] In general, they do this by correlating what is *said* with all the information that is available to anyone who has been raised in our particular culture—that is, with cultural norms—as well as other personal information they may have in hand. The mind is like Velcro—new stuff has to connect with the loops that are already there or it simply slides off and gets lost.

## Listeners Connect the Dots by Looking for Resonance with Other Truth

British literary critic Northrup Frye calls this capacity for making connections *resonance*. We look for reasonable connections with other parts of what we know, and then we use those reasonable connections as resources for filling in the gaps in information. One can say that we listen for resonance between what we already know and what we're hearing. It's resonance, says Frye, that enables something particular to acquire universal or metaphorical significance. In the book of Isaiah, the phrase "grapes of wrath" is a celebration of the impending massacre of the Edomites, but because of resonance, the phrase, "has long ago flown away from this context to new contexts, contexts that give dignity to the human situation instead of merely reflecting its bigotries."[4]

According to Frye, it is resonance that enables a place like Athens to acquire universal significance as a type and symbol of great learning and art, or Jerusalem to come to symbolize humanity's great struggle for redemption:

> The smallest details of geography of two tiny chopped-up countries, Greece and Israel, have imposed themselves on our consciousness until they have become part of our own imaginative world, whether we have ever seen these countries or not.[5]

When the African-American slave sang the old spiritual, "I'm goin' to cross over into Canaan," the imagery of the Hebrew children leaving bondage in Egypt and crossing over into the Promised Land resonated with the dream of freedom in the north. "Canaan" came to symbolize Canada, or perhaps any place north of the Mason-Dixon Line.

The human capacity to find resonance is closely connected to our ability to identify patterns. In a restaurant near my home the walls are painted with what appear at first to be random shapes:

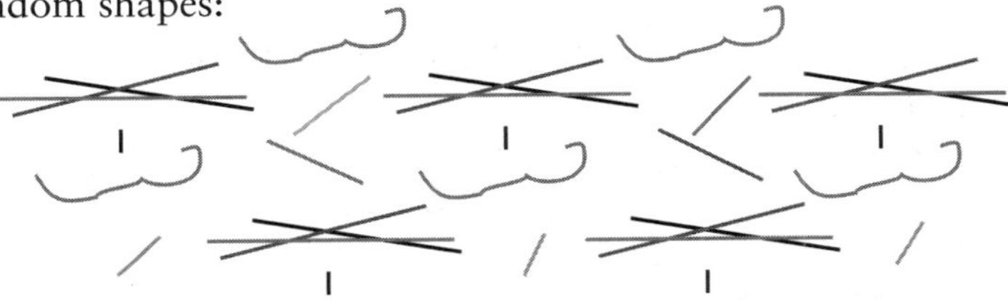

It took me a half-bowl of clam chowder before I realized that the random lines were actually faces painted on the wall.

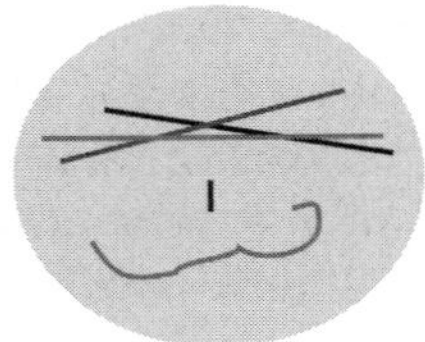

This one seems obvious, but it wasn't at first because the lines were painted in different colors. Once I had seen a single face, all of the others seemed to slide glibly into view. Some were winking, some scowling, some laughing. I left the restaurant without having dessert because I felt I had had already been given a tasty enough visual treat.

The faces in the lines were partly the work of the artist, and partly my own doing. If I was going to see them, I had to work to find the right patterns and relationships that were there but disguised by the color scheme. We do that sort of work all of the time, even though we are not consciously aware of it. At the university where I teach I sometimes have a deep sense of resonance with some student, and it may take me an hour or more to realize that in the face of the student I am seeing the face of a parent with whom I went to school. The clues, disguised by youth and subtle differences of DNA, still are there, and I make the connections before I'm consciously aware that I have done so.

Sometimes our pattern making can get us into trouble. We read some medical journal and discover that we, too, have all of these diseases and for the next several months we just *know* we are dying.

Sometimes it can be very helpful. The year 1988 was a very difficult year for me. I experienced a failed attempt at promotion (though I did receive tenure, thank you very much). The failed bid for promotion coincided with a series of flashbacks of repressed memories of childhood violence. I know now that the decision of the promotion committee was resonating with the childhood violence, but I only know this in retrospect. Like intersecting waves on a pond, the two very different experiences deepened each other's troughs, so there were times when I was very discouraged. For more than a year I was hurt and angry, and I felt a deep sense of public humiliation.

Then something odd happened. Our next-door neighbors, Sue and Dave, had a baby. Shaleen and I agreed that we would take in their children while they went to the hospital, and so we found ourselves parenting five kids for the weekend. Sue and Dave were gone for what seemed like a week. The longer we waited the greater became our sense of concern. Eventually, Dave called. "It's a boy," he said. And then he told us this:

> "We had a terrible delivery. After nearly 50 hours of labor, Sue was only dilated to two centimeters. (Natural childbirth requires a dilation of 10.) But she was exhausted, so the doctor made an executive decision and took the baby by Caesarean section. When he did, we discovered that the umbilical cord had been wrapped around the baby's neck. Had he moved down the birth canal, he would have suffered irreparable brain damage, or perhaps even died from the lack of oxygen. This is what the doctor said to Sue: 'Your long struggle probably saved your baby's life.' "

This is what was odd: After that, I was somehow better able to handle the long struggle I was going through with my problems at work. I had managed to find *resonance* between Sue's story and my own, and to hear her doctor's words in a way that lifted my own spirits from a moment of dismay.

### The Hermeneutic of Everyday Life—Resonating with Each Other

The resonances that play in the daily music of the gossip are also key factors in building up our basic assumptions about life and how it works, or how it *ought* to work. When my bid for promotion failed I triangled a good many friends who I hoped would see things from my perspective and offer consolation. When they responded in ways that told me that they *resonated* with my sense of grief and loss, I knew I wasn't alone. When they were put off, or when they didn't resonate the way I hoped, my sense of alienation deepened.

This leads to the observation that in matters of our personal worth we tend to feel safer with those who approve of our way of telling the story. Put another way, the resonances are major factors by which we learn the hermeneutic of everyday life that we discussed in chapter 4. Remember that the hermeneutic of everyday life is the pattern of interpretation that guides the movement from *event* to *story.* Linguistics professor George Lakoff and philosophy professor Mark Johnson explore this topic in terms of the root metaphors that drive the ways we actually live our lives—"down to the most mundane details."[6] "The essence of metaphor," say Lakoff and Johnson, "is understanding and experiencing one kind of thing in terms of another,"[7] in other words, by resonance. We can discover the root metaphors around which a group organizes its daily life by listening to the nuances of its language when it is spoken casually. For example, the fact that English speakers often orient their day around the root metaphor, *time is money*, is evident in the ways we talk about the business of life:

- "You're *wasting* my time."
- "This gadget will *save* you hours."
- "How do you *spend* your time these days?"
- "That flat tire *cost* me an hour."
- "I've *invested* a lot of time in her."
- "You need to *budget* your time."
- "He's living on *borrowed* time."
- "You don't *use* your time *profitably*."

There are two reasons for repeating this discussion here. First, it is clear that the root metaphors of our culture have profound effects on our spiritual lives not only because they form the environment within which we have to live out our spirituality, but also because they define for us what that spirituality must be. If I believe that *time is money*, I may be inclined to evaluate my prayer time in terms of its efficiency, or to judge the value of time spent in worship in terms of measurable outcomes, rather than as activities done for their own sake.

It is important that different cultures and subcultures engage such questions in different ways. The root metaphors reflect very different hermeneutics of everyday life. Consider the root metaphors for education. In the subculture of the university, those root metaphors could be summarized as *education is power,* or *education is freedom.* Outside of the university there may be very different root metaphors for education, with very different ways for organizing and telling the stories of everyday life, and consequently, very different social effects.

One afternoon I was approached in a coffee shop by an elderly stranger who wanted to talk. Apparently he had heard I was a minister, and he needed some help coming to terms with his sense of loss over his career when he retired. For many years he had taught sixth grade in one of our county's poorer school districts, a job he found both satisfying and frustrating. The frustrations, he said, were often over cultural differences. Most of the students in that school district were from a culture that did not put much value on education. In the terms we are developing in this discussion, they had a different root metaphor for education.

"Tell me about the frustrations," I said.

"That's the odd thing," he said to me. "When these kids didn't do well, I often had the impression that it wasn't because they couldn't, or even that they didn't want to. I had the impression that they were afraid to do well."

"Afraid?" I asked. "Why would they be afraid?"

"Once I had this boy," he said. "Good boy. Smart, too. Grades were B+, A-. When I handed out the report cards, he started to cry. 'What's the matter,' I asked. 'Aren't your grades good enough?" 'No,' he said. 'They're too good. They're better than my father would have gotten. If he sees these, he'll beat me.'"

"What did you do?" I asked.

"I made the boy a bogus report card to take home for his father's signature. It had C's and D's on it, which served just fine."

When I reported this encounter to a class at the university, my students did not believe that I was telling the truth. Then a young woman named Alana spoke up in the back of the room. She was from the same culture as the boy in the story.

"This really happened," she said. "I know because something like it happened to me. I'm the first woman in my family ever to go to college. My brothers and sisters won't have anything to do with me."

Here, I thought (reflecting my own culture's root metaphor, *education is freedom*) were children whose families had constructed little prisons for them to live in. To be fair, I should point out that their root metaphor for education makes its own kind of sense. When this young lady went away to college, the one thing her family knew for certain was that she would never move back to her old neighborhood. Their disdain for her education was a strategy for keeping her close to home, friends, and family. The backroom gossip by which they talked about her being altogether too uppity was an expression of their grief that the strategy would not work.

## To Join a Group We Must Adopt the Hermeneutic by Which Its Members Tell Their Stories

As the experience of my student Alana illustrates, when we leave one social group and join another, we must sometimes learn an alien hermeneutic and adopt a different vocabulary to go with it. Like John J. Dunbar, Alana was learning a new language and adopting a new tribe. When she returns to visit her family she may also learn the ironic truth that an improved vocabulary can inhibit communication. If she can find the range and grace within herself, she will learn that she can be a member of two tribes only by being consciously bilingual.

How are such things taught or learned? No teacher I ever had instructed his or her students that they must not do better than their fathers. I do not remember ever reading a formal argument that time is money. We do not learn such things in school. We learn them in the daily conversation that permeates everything else. Out of that daily talk, our gossip, we build up a world of root metaphors—ideas about what's good and what's bad, what's valuable, what's not, what's worthy of our attention, what's a waste of our time.

### Resonance, Root Metaphors, and the Spiritual Journey

It seems clear that resonance is a central part of the whole business of coffee shop gossip. It's resonance that enables us to go about injustice collecting ("I know exactly what you mean, he did the same thing to me once!"), and resonance that enables us to connect our contribution to the developing thread of the conversation. Resonance is also a factor in the believability of a story we tell. The telling must "ring true"—it must *resonate with*—the root metaphors that listeners take for granted as they come to terms with life by telling and hearing stories. Resonance is what makes the *Chicken Soup for the Soul* books so successful: In the homely details of tiny moments, in their very particularity, these little stories somehow resonate with what we sense must be universal themes.

It is difficult to overestimate the enormous significance resonance and root metaphors have on the decisions that most profoundly affect our spiritual lives. In *The Urban Christian*, seminary professor Ray Bakke describes the moment at which he knew his vocation for ministry would be to the world's cities. He had been reading Hugh Moule's biography of Charles Simeon (1759-1836), who was appointed vicar of Holy Trinity Church in Cambridge, England. When Simeon became vicar, the congregation was made up of a tiny group of the city's elites, huddled together against the world. Meanwhile, profound social changes in the countryside had left the slums outside the church teeming with the city's poor. Simeon began a campaign to bring the gospel into the slum, and the poor into the church. The members were outraged, and for eleven years they protested to the bishop, locked their pews against the poor, and hired their own lecturer so they would not have to listen to this upstart and offensive evangelist.

In the twelfth year, something broke in the congregation, the walls came down, and there was revival. Out of that revival came Inter-Varsity, the Cambridge Seven, a mission to China, and a flood of evangelists who worked to transform the inner cities of England. Bakke's description of his own call to ministry is a classic demonstration that the Holy Spirit can use something so simple as the human capacity for resonance to bring about deep spiritual transformation:

> As I read Moule's biography, I began to feel I was a kindred spirit with these people who had been concerned with urban-mission issues more than a hundred years ago. I knew my life was being changed.[8]

## *Schadenfreude* and Stories of Payback

The other side of the resonance coin is something the Germans know as *Schadenfreude*—the secret pleasure we take when someone else gets into trouble. Schadenfreude accounts for our delight in trickster stories and stories of payback. There's a wonderful little story of payback circulating in the town where I live.

It appears that the police were called one day to the scene of an accident near the local high school. When the police officer arrived, though, there was no accident in sight. Instead there was a crew working on the road. He pulled his cruiser over and asked the supervisor about the call.

"I made the call," said the supervisor.

"Where's the accident?" asked the police officer.

"It hasn't happened yet."

"Do you want to explain that to me?" asked the police officer.

"Sure," said the supervisor. "It's like this. Every afternoon when school gets out the kids come streaming out of that driveway over there. One of them drives a brand-new Jeep Wrangler. Every day when he pulls out, he drives right down the safety cones. It's not only annoying, it's dangerous. My men could get hurt. I've warned him a half dozen times, and he just laughs and the next day does it again. So this is what I've done. I've filled those first three cones with concrete. When he hits the first one, it's going to take out his radiator. The second cone will take out his front axle and his differential. I called you here early so you could watch the whole thing and write up a report as a first-hand observer. Why don't you pull your cruiser out of sight around that corner, and watch. There's a good view from behind that tree."

According to the story, the police officer did just that.

Payback stories are like that. The little guy finally takes down the giant corporation. Wiley tricks the Hairy Man. (It's not by accident that he's named "Wiley.") We experience a secret Schadenfreude when the gossip columns expose the human frailties of our bigger than life media moguls or our politicians. Somehow when we learn that an immensely wealthy Howard Hughes was paranoid, we don't feel so bad about not having much money of our own. There's satisfaction in Schadenfreude. (The exact German phrase is, *Schadenfreude ist die schönste Freude*—"Schadenfreude is the most *exquisite* joy!") The satisfaction, I believe, is a good example of resonance. We savor the moment when the police officer writes up his report and somehow it strikes a chord with our own experience; in some odd way, we feel that we ourselves have struck a blow for justice.

Perhaps that's why peasant societies love to gossip about tricksters. Peasants, after all, are often marginalized and powerless. Where there is a sense of helplessness about ever seeing justice done, tricksters are the ones who know how to even the score. Indeed, both the Bible itself and the literature from between the testaments are filled with trickster stories for precisely this reason, a fact that provides indirect evidence that Jewish culture was a culture produced under the pressure-cooker of trouble.

Even today, the folklore of the Middle East is filled with stories about tricksters. One such fellow is named Nasrudin. Sometimes Nasrudin is a fat man, and sometimes he is skinny. In some of the stories he's a wealthy man, and in others he's poor, but always he is a trickster.

One day Nasrudin went to the public bathhouse in Istanbul. In this telling of the story, he is a poor man, very dirty. The attendant met him at the door with a look of disgust.

"Go away, Nasrudin," he said. "You are too dirty to take a bath." What he meant was that he did not want to clean the pool afterward.

"But I have money," said Nasrudin. "Money like everyone else. I will pay for the bath. Indeed, there is even something here for you." He shook aloft his coin purse, and sure enough, it rattled.

"Very well," said the attendant, "but not here in these pools. These are reserved for customers who are less trouble than you will be. Go down that hallway to the last door. Turn right and go to the last pool. It is very dirty still—I have not cleaned it yet—but you will not add much to the dirt. You can dry yourself with these rags." Without losing his scowl, he handed Nasrudin some threadbare towels and thrust his chin in the direction of the end of the hallway.

Some time later Nasrudin came out, scrubbed raw, but clean. He met the attendant at the door.

"Here," he said, "this is for you." Reaching into his coin purse he drew out a large gold coin, which he waved appreciatively in the attendant's astonished eyes, and placed in the extended white-gloved hand.

You can imagine the treatment he received when he appeared the following week. The attendant stood at stiff attention, clicked his heels, and addressed Nasrudin by the honorific title, "mullah."

"Good morning, Nasrudin, mullah, excellency. I have reserved a fine pool for you today. Here in the front. The water is hot and steaming. If you will give me your shoes I will have the boy polish them for you. Here are three fresh towels. Call me when you are ready and I will see that you are properly rubbed down! Excellency!"

And so Nasrudin ran the man ragged for the rest of the morning.

When he finally dressed to leave, he stopped by the door and took out his coin purse. The attendant stood at attention, gloved hand extended. Into the glove, Nasrudin placed a small copper coin, worth about a penny.

"This is for you," he said.

"But what is this?" asked the attendant, now just as astonished as he had been the week before.

"*This* is for *last* week. *That* was for *this* week."

**To Sum Up**

These, then, are among the reasons why adults listen to gossip—resonance with our own experience, the curiosity raised by deviations from cultural norms and root metaphors, and Schadenfreude. If we gossip to gather useful information about a changing social situation, we will attend to the elements of the gossip that are new, interesting, or threatening. If we gossip for the pleasures of Schadenfreude, those pleasures themselves will be factors in the listening process. All of these in one way or another impinge on the management of power. If we cannot manage power in our real life, we will manage it in our language, and that shapes not only what we are likely to say, but also what we are likely to hear.

Here, also is an explanation for what happened with Lori

and David and the story of the princess who lived in a prison. As the story developed, Lori found a point of entry in the resonance between the plight of the princess and her own inner experience of being entrapped in a prison of her own. It was a good fit, and in some sense she must have come to think that I had told the story just for her. The problem was, the story ran beyond her. She had not yet come to the place where she was able to say to her therapist what the princess had said to the traveler: "There. It's gone. I don't live there any more."

So she felt bullied and exposed, and in her panic she went home and triangled David. Fair enough. But David didn't take into account Lori's state of mind when she told him the story, and so he filled the gaps in the story line in a particular way. His gap filling presupposed not only that what she had told him was true, but also that it was the whole truth. That's why I found him pounding on my door, ready to pummel me for humiliating his wife in public!

Luckily, David and Lori did decide to come confront me and we were able to clear up the matter. Imagine all the people who, like Lori, personally enter into someone's gossip, are shamed and hurt, and never return to clear things up. Imagine all the wounds that are festering because someone *heard* wrongly.

There is a curious epilogue to this little story. As Lori and David stood to leave, Lori turned and looked me full in the eye. This was an uncharacteristic move for her.

"One more thing you should know," she said. "Your face has my father's bone structure. My father used to beat me when I was a child."

"Thank you, Lori," I said. What I was thanking her for was a point of entry into her story, a peephole through which I could enter empathically into her experience. Lori's story resonated with my own childhood, and her comment made sense to me about why she would be doubtful about my motives.

Still, before the day was done, I found a thoughtful colleague and shared with him what had happened. As I talked I took care, as I have done now, to tell the story in such a way that I would come out looking like a decent fellow who had been misunderstood. I did this, I freely admit, because I needed his reassurance that this episode of near violence would come out all right in the end, and I would not be left alone should something like it happen again.

CHAPTER SIX

# SEEN AND NOT HEARD

## Educating Our Children by Accident

*The emotions of prejudice are formed in early childhood, while the beliefs that are used to justify it come later. . . . Later in life you may want to change your prejudice, but it is far easier to change your intellectual beliefs than your deep feelings.*
—Thomas Pettigrew

Let's open this chapter with a scene whose primary actor is my son Jonathan, who is four years old when this takes place. He and I are engaged in a little experiment on the kitchen counter. I've set three glass objects on the counter—two identical short, squat juice glasses, and a tall thin glass cylinder I borrowed from the chemistry lab at the university. The two juice glasses are filled to the brim with water.

"Jonathan," I say. "Can you tell me which of the glasses has more water?"

"They have the same amount, Daddy."

Good job so far. I then pour the contents of one of the glasses into the tall cylinder.

"Now which?"

"The tall one has more water than the short one."

Then I pour the water back into the short glass.

"Now?"

"Now they have the same amount of water again."

If Jonathan had been older, this answer would have been ridiculous, even comical, but for a four-year-old it made good sense. At that age, he had not yet mastered the rather complex developmental tasks necessary to understand the principle that a change of shape doesn't require a change of quantity. That principle required that he be able to envision both form and substance at the same time, and to know that a change in one did not require a change in the other. Since he did not understand that principle, he lived in a world that had to work without it.

Of course, this is not the only piece of information Jonathan was living without. There are thousands of principles and hundreds of thousands of pieces of orienting information that he is mastering on his journey to adulthood. Even cause and effect must be learned, either by instruction or discovery. But what is the world like for children before they make that journey? Since their understandings cannot take into account the things they don't yet know or cannot yet grasp, they're left with a world that's put together by what seems like magic. Things happen, they sometimes don't know why, and the things that happen are not always understood as safe. The magic doesn't always work out the way the child wanted. The journey to adulthood involves mastery of this magical and sometimes frightening world.

This is not only so of the child's sense of the world outside, but also of the child's sense of his or her interior life. What is the child to do with feelings like frustration? Elation? Fear? Rage? How does a young boy come to terms with the conflicting feelings of pleasure and embarrassment the first time a girl "speaks to his blood," to borrow a graphic phrase from my father's vocabulary? How does a young girl manage her feelings of awkwardness when no one asks her to the dance, or she doesn't get that expected invitation to the sleepover?

In a larger sense, how does a child learn that time is money or that education is freedom or that children must not get better grades than their fathers?

Somehow we all seem to muddle through these experiences, but how do we muddle through? What resources do we draw upon to inform and shape our muddling? It is the contention of this chapter that gossip plays an important role in the muddling process. Not the only role, mind you. There are thousands of other contributing factors—baseball games, roller hockey, burned biscuits, rap sessions with friends, late homework, chores, Bible studies, the example set by friends, the example set by parents, the time Bobby stayed up late and missed an exam. But in the mix, gossip plays an important role. There are three reasons why this is so.

### Parental Talk Is Apprenticeship Talk

First, gossip is everywhere. By that I mean that it's carried on all the time, without the structures that control formal instruction and learning. The child's earliest learning is learning by overhearing. Much of the emotional content children will later attach to their social experiences will be formed in that tentative just-learning-to-talk stage when they understand more than they can say.

There's something important about the informality of it all. Formal instruction invites the child to learn on the teacher's timetable, while gossip allows the child to learn as occasions present themselves. Gossip is education about life on an apprenticeship model. It's more accessible to the child, with more fluidity, more give-and-take. As children listen to their parents talk at the table, they learn about life without being aware that they are learning about life.

### Parental Talk Teaches Children What's Coming Next . . .

Second, from listening to their parents talk children learn how to interpret what happens to them, and what consequences to expect from different kinds of behaviors.

Stephen Covey, author of *The Seven Habits of Highly Effective People*, describes a transforming experience on a New York subway:

People were sitting quietly, some reading newspapers, some lost in thought, and others simply resting with their eyes closed. It was a calm and peaceful Sunday morning scene. Suddenly, a man entered the subway car with several children who were so loud and rambunctious that instantly the peaceful atmosphere disappeared and the whole climate changed.

The man sat down next to Covey and closed his eyes, apparently oblivious to the situation around him. The children, meanwhile, were yelling, throwing things, and even grabbing people's papers. Their behavior was disturbing, and yet, the man, their father did nothing.

Covey writes that he found it difficult to not feel irritated. We pick up the story where he decides to speak to the father:

> So finally, with what I felt was unusual patience and restraint, I turned to him and said, "Sir, your children are really disturbing a lot of people. I wonder if you couldn't control them a little more?"
>
> The man lifted his gaze as if to come to a consciousness of the situation for the first time and said softly, "Oh, you're right. I guess I should do something about it. We just came from the hospital where their mother died about an hour ago. I don't know what to think, and I guess they don't know how to handle it either."
>
> Can you imagine what I felt at that moment? My paradigm shifted. Suddenly I saw things differently, and because I saw differently, I thought differently, I felt differently, I behaved differently. My irritation vanished. I didn't have to worry about controlling my attitude or my behavior; my heart was filled with the man's pain. . . . Everything changed in an instant.[1]

But this could very well have gone a different direction. Imagine instead that Covey had turned to his wife and said—in the hearing of his own children—"If those kids were mine, I'd beat the daylights out of them!" How would his children have understood this cutting remark? How would it have shaped their understanding of themselves, and their own inner confusions and difficulties? Would a moment in which they could have learned to be more compassionate not somehow have turned upon itself and become a moment of violence in its own right?

Or what of the young teenage daughter who overhears her mother tell Mrs. Grimm from church, "Oh! I just knew that Smith girl was a tramp. If my Janie ever did something like that, her father would disown her." Maybe this will make the young eavesdropper think twice before getting into the backseat with her boyfriend, but should the unfortunate happen, she may be driven to desperate measures in an abortion clinic or worse. Anything not to have to tell her mother and face the consequences. For better or for worse, parental talk teaches children about consequences.

### Parental Talk Helps Children Connect . . . or *Dis*connect

The third reason these little third party conversations play a central role in the child's development is that they form important points of connection with, or disconnection from, the child's parents and other caregivers. When I was a boy of perhaps eight years old I had one of those unforgettable, very painful conversations with my father. We were building forms for the foundation of a new educational wing for the church. In the background a rock song came on the radio. I snapped my fingers to the rhythm of the music.

"Cut that out," my father said. "You don't want to sound like no big sweatin' black man, do you?"

In what my father was saying, and in the diction he chose—he used a stronger term than black man—he was drawing lines between *them* and *us*.

"What would be wrong with that?" I asked.

"They're no example to copy. They're inferior in every way. No white man with any self-respect wants to look or act like a black man."

"How do you get that?" I asked.

"It's there in the Bible," my father said. "Sons of Cain, marked for servitude. Bible says it's so, and I believe it. That's why they're so stupid. And they're lazy, too. The Bible says they're supposed to be the servants and slaves of white men. It's just the way it is. But now they're trying to take our jobs away. Do white man's work. Isn't right."

"You're going to have to make up your mind," I said to my father. "Either they're inferior, or they are not. If they're inferior, then you should have no problem allowing them to compete with you for a job in the workplace. If you think they can take your job from you, then you cannot also think they're inferior. It has to be one way or the other, but it can't be both."

This was a deciding conversation of my childhood, and I have reported it here just the way I remember it. My father's recollection is no doubt quite different. With this conversation, I disconnected from my father and made up my mind to look elsewhere for a mentor and role model. Perhaps more importantly, in this conversation I embraced a stance on equal rights that I have held for all of my adult life.

But this occasion also created an important connection with someone else. My father was angry that I would respond to him this way, and he took me by the ear and hauled me into Pastor Marshall's office.

"Pastor," he said. "Tell this boy that black people are supposed to be the servants and slaves of white people. It's in the Bible, pastor, and he'll believe it if it comes from you."

"What's this about?" asked Pastor Marshall.

So my father told his side of the story, and then I told mine. This presented the pastor with a dilemma because my father was a prominent man in our church. What he said next was risky, but he said it because he was a man of principle.

"You know," he said, "the boy's right."

That was the moment that I discovered that Gordon Marshall was a man of courage and honesty, and the example he set is one I have tried to live up to all of my life. We did not become friends, but later in life he made it a point to be present to hear me preach my first sermon, and several years after that his family asked me to officiate at his funeral. Several weeks after Pastor Marshall's funeral I was called out of a faculty meeting to sign for a large, heavy package from his wife, Elizabeth. It was his pulpit Bible, and it occupies a place of great honor on a special stand in my study. It is a holy object to me.

## Parental Talk Teaches Children About Faith . . . and Faithlessness

Harvard professor Sharon Parks tells a smaller, more poignant tale of connections and disconnections from childhood caregivers. The key actor in the story is an unnamed six-year-old girl.

> This little girl was being tucked into bed in another in a much too long line of foster homes by yet one more temporary "mother." The new foster mother was surprised when the little girl asked her to take off her wedding ring so she could see it. But wanting to respond warmly to the little girl, she did as requested, and then was startled when the little girl clutched the ring tightly and putting her little fist firmly under her pillow she said, "There. Now you won't leave me while I'm sleeping."[2]

Let Sharon Parks' comment on this story serve as a general commentary on the whole range of conversations we have with our children, and with other people in the presence of our children. Let it serve as well as a comment on Pastor Marshall's pulpit Bible in my study:

> I invite us as educators concerned with the formation of faith to recognize that the central issues of faith were at stake for that little girl—belief and doubt, promise and betrayal, power and powerlessness, belonging and exclusion, suffering and hope. That little girl represents the dialectic of faith—and not just because she is a child. She knew the ring to be precious to the adult, primarily because of its power to touch the adult experience of belief and doubt, promise and betrayal, power and powerlessness, belonging and exclusion, suffering and hope.[3]

And how, one wonders, do children learn such things? They learn them, I contend, far more profoundly in the things we say about other people when we think our children are not listening, than in the things we say to them by way of direct instruction or teaching. Children learn such things by tuning in to their parents as they gossip.

CHAPTER SEVEN

# TICKLED EARS, TICKLED FANCIES

## Coming Face to Face with the Hairy Man

*Just as his life is often bewildering to him, the child needs even more to be given the chance to understand himself in the complex world in which he must learn to cope. To be able to do this, the child must be helped to make some coherent sense out of the turmoil of his feelings. He needs ideas on how to bring his inner house into order.*

—Bruno Bettelheim

In chapter 5 we explored some of the factors that influence the ways adults listen to the gossip at the water cooler, namely, resonance with our own experience, schadenfreude, and the management of power. Children are influenced by these same factors. Just as for adults, the reasons children listen, influence what they hear. Except with children, the work of childhood involves a different set of challenges and different resources for meeting them.

What, exactly, are the children doing as they listen to the gossip around the dinner table? What motives and skills do they bring to the listening? To answer such questions, it is helpful to ask why and how children listen to the more carefully crafted stories found in the published children's literature, such as folktales and fairy tales. Why do children want to hear the same story over and over again? What keeps them listening even after they've heard a story umpteen times? (If I could find a cure for this condition and bottle it, I could make a small mint.)

A story is rather like an airplane that spirits the child away on an imaginary adventure—something has to keep it up in the air. The child's imagination is what gives it wings, but what are the engines that pull it forward? It is important that there are more engines than one. If the child's mind were like a single engine Cessna, any distraction or interruption would disrupt the attention span and the story would crash and burn. But if there were more than one engine—say, like a DC-10—then if one of the engines went out, there would still be enough forward thrust for the story to continue to fly. Children continue to listen because of the certain pleasures they experience in the listening.

**Children Listen to the Sounds**

The first engine is the pleasure the child takes in the sheer *sounds* of the stories, what we called aural texture in chapter 3. The sounds may have a soothing, melodic effect, as they do, for example, in the bedtime story, *Goodnight Moon*, by Margaret Wise Brown:

> In the great green room
> There was a telephone
> And a red balloon . . .
> And a comb and a brush
> And a bowl full of mush
> And a quiet old lady
> Who was whispering "hush."[1]

When I tell "Wiley and the Hairy Man," I always give the Hairy Man a deep, gravelly, throaty voice. He nearly barks or growls when he talks to Wiley: "Whatchu doin' in here, boy?" A Hairy Man with a gravelly voice is somehow *hairier* than a Hairy Man without one.

## Children Listen for the Pictures

Children also take a certain pleasure in the *visual* images the stories allow them to create in their imaginations. This is the second engine that drives the child's attention. I discovered the importance of this aspect of storytelling during my son's fourth grade trip to the California state capital in Sacramento. We were in the airport for the trip home; the kids were tired, the parents were distracted, and the airport noise was nearly deafening. Clearly what was needed was a story. We found a corner where all 160 of us could huddle together out of the flow of traffic, and I told the story of "Sir Gawain and the Loathly Lady." The operative word here is "loathly." It doesn't take a genius to realize that so far as a fourth grader is concerned, the grosser the image the better.

We pick up the story as King Arthur is riding out to meet the Black Knight for a battle of wits—he has to answer a riddle, for which he has no clue—when he is distracted by a shift in the wind. The wind carried the most foul odor he had ever smelled, and a sound that was almost like singing (he wasn't sure it was a human sound at all). When the king turned in the direction of the wind, he saw an old woman, seated on a boulder near a small thicket of reeds.

She had gray matted hair that looked like it had never been washed or brushed, but she was balding at the top, so you could see age spots showing through where her hair thinned. Her right eye was swollen shut, and her left eye was rubbed raw and running fluid out of the corner, down the left side of her cheek. Her nose was broken in two places. She had horses' teeth, yellow and crooked like a broken down picket fence. The teeth were so long she couldn't quite close her mouth as she sang, so she drooled onto her chin, where there were open, running sores.

In a doubled-up chicken claw she held a long staff. She was wearing leathers, and from the layers of sweat stains, the king knew that it had been a very long time since the leathers had been off her or cleaned. He guessed that the stench must be coming from the leathers.

Those fourth grade students are now in high school, and still when they see me they ask me to tell them again about the "Loathly Lady." What they remember is not the *words* of the story, but the sheer loathliness of her, a loathliness brought back by the graphic images the story invited them to picture in their minds.

This is true of the Wiley story, too. The Hairy Man really *is* hairy. The following clip comes just as the Hairy Man has grabbed Wiley by the nape of the neck.

> He turned him around, and Wiley found hisself lookin' at the hairiest man he had ever seen in alla his life. Had brownish, yellowish, grayish, blackish kinda hair. Hairy Man was wearin' overalls, and no shirt, and he had hair on his shoulders. Wiley could see hair on his toes. Hairy Man was one o' those kinda men who never shaves, so his beard fell down nearly to his belly button, and worse of all, it crept up over his cheeks, so when Wiley looked at him all he could see was hair, and eyeballs, and . . . teeth.

## Children Listen for What's Coming Next . . . and Next After That

The third and most obvious engine that drives the child's attention to the story is curiosity about what's going to happen next, and then next after that. In the story of Wiley and the Hairy Man, several questions form up in the child's mind as the story develops. Will there really be a Hairy Man in the swamp? Does he really want to eat Wiley up? Will Wiley be able to outrun him? Beat him off? Outwit him? How? Hairy Man speaks first:

"Whachu doin' in here, boy?"

"I'm on a errand for my mama. She asked me to carry these things over to my grampa's house that lives on the other side o' the swamp. I'd best be goin', cause he's spectin' me. After all, iss almose suppertime." *At this point in the telling, I slow the word "suppertime" down almost to a hiss—"s-u-p-p-e-r-t-i-m-e." Wiley's hesitating. He didn't mean to remind the Hairy Man about that.*

"I knows iss almose suppertime cuz I's hungry."

"I got a idea, Mr. Hairy Man. Why don't I tell my grampa you's in here and he can come give you somethin' to eat." *Wiley's in a near panic now, but he keeps his composure; the panic shows in his voice, which is now strained to a high pitch.*

"Cuz I's hungry *now.*" *Slow and emphatic on the "now."*

"I got a idea, Mr. Hairy Man. Inside my knapsack here I got three jars o' jelly and two loaves o' my mama's fresh-baked bread. They'd make a mighty fine supper."

"Ain't hungry for jelly and bread. I's hungry for *BOY!*"

And he picked Wiley up and held him over his head. Threw his head back to swallow Wiley all in one piece. Wiley found hisself lookin' down between his ankles at hair, and eyeballs, and . . . teeth.

At this point the story cuts to the farmhouse, where Wiley's Mama is in the kitchen, peeling apples "on account of she was makin' apple pie for Wiley on account of she was so proud of him cuz he was bein' so brave and all." The cut to the farmhouse leaves the child hanging. Mamas can do anything, but how will she know Wiley's in trouble? Will she get there in time?

This curiosity about what will happen next is somehow close to the heart of what makes a story engaging. A series of events without some sort of trouble isn't really a story at all, but just a series of events. It takes trouble to make a plot. In literary terms, we say that the plot *complicates.* Wiley meets the Hairy Man and things turn ugly. The crisis comes at the moment Wiley "finds hisself lookin' down between his ankles at hair and eyeballs, and . . . teeth."

### Children Get Inside the Story by Identifying with Characters

The fourth, and by far the most important, engine that engages the child's attention is identification with characters. Identification is the ability to "climb inside the skin" of some character and view the story as though it's happening to *me*. Identification with characters is an important form of resonance.

Let's return for a moment to an earlier place in the story of Wiley and the Hairy Man. Wiley, you will recall, has been sent by his mother on an errand that takes him through the Yellow Belly Swamp. Wiley has already told his mama he's scared of the Hairy Man, "the one that lives up in the swamp and wantsa eat me up." But Mama insists, and Wiley is a good boy, so off he goes.

One of the things I like about telling this story to groups of little children is watching their eyes widen as the road turns left—"straight into the middle of the swamp." Here I slow the story down deliberately, and I let my breath get heavy and quiet, almost to a whisper. The deeper Wiley goes in the swamp, the darker the shadows get. And the larger the eyes of the audience get, too. There's always a hush. When Wiley hears footsteps on the gravel road behind him, the children almost stop breathing. That's when I ask, "You know how it is when you're alone in a swamp and there's a Hairy Man in there wantsa eat you up?" And every single child nods his or her head. I've been telling this story for nearly twenty years, and every single child *knows* what it's like to be alone in a swamp when there's a Hairy Man in there. But they don't really know that. What they know is how they would feel if they were themselves alone in a swamp, and they know how *that* feels because they've identified with Wiley as a way of entering into the story. On some deep psychological level, identification allows the imaginary dangers in the story to resonate with the child's deeper, less accessible fears.

What interests us here is the capacity to see the world through someone else's eyes, since that capacity explains a variety of psychological interactions we have with narratives at all levels. Because language is selective, the characters will naturally be underdeveloped. This native feature of language provides the child with the elbow room that's necessary if he or she is to squeeze inside of Wiley and feel what it is like to move deeper and deeper into a swamp. It's what George Poulet once called "a magical ability that allows the interiority of one human being to play host to the interiority of another."[2]

### To Sum Up Thus Far

There are, then, four basic engines that drive the listening process forward:

- *Children like the rhythm and meter of the story,* the gooeyness, the smoothness, or the roughness of the storyteller's voice.
- *They like to picture the story*, and the more vivid the image, the more satisfying the story.
- *They worry about what will happen next*, and then next after that.
- *They identify with characters;* they pretend the story is about them.

Each of these four things contributes its own lines to the map the child follows as he or she makes the difficult journey of mastery of the world, on the way to adulthood.

### Listening and Learning

*Sound* forms an important point of entry to memory. Think of how you try and reconstruct the lyric of some long forgotten song. Tune, rhyme, rhythm, and meter all rest on top of the primary content of the lyric, so we have two or three windows to the deeper recesses of the mind. We work the windows together, tapping the rhythm with our fingers, humming the melody under our breath, until—voila!—we arrive home, lyric in hand. What this means is that sound is a factor in learning, and therefore one of the primary means children use to store and retrieve what we are teaching them.

*Visual memory* is also an important part of the child's learning processes. Once, while I was standing on the bluff of Masada, I asked the guide a question about Capernaum, a site several hours drive to the north. She did a strange thing—she gazed straight ahead, focusing about five or six inches in front of her. She held this gaze for perhaps ten seconds, then she returned to me and answered my question. When I asked her where she "went" during her little trance, she said this: "I'm usually asked that question at Capernaum itself. I pictured myself standing on the site of the synagogue there, I looked around me at all of the visual reminders I usually draw upon, and there I found the answer to the question you asked. Then I came back here to tell you."

In physical truth, she had not "gone" anywhere at all; what happened was that she took an imaginary ride through one of the portals of her mind to the place where she stored a particular piece of information. Visual memory is like that. Like sound, visual images provide an important pathway into the memory. Ask your grandfather a loose, unstructured question about the halcyon days of his youth—"Grampa, tell me 'bout the good ole days"—and you're likely to get a blank stare. But ask him to tell you about the old homestead on Maple Street where he and Gramma lived right after they first got married, and his eyes will mist over, and he'll remember the slapping of the screen door, and the tree where Uncle Jimmy broke his leg, and the free standing garage with his old farm truck parked inside, and then, on the heels of the visual images, the stories will begin to flow.

*Curiosity about what happens* and why it happens also stands at the center of the child's drive to learn about life. By watching what happens next, and then next after that, the child learns about cause and effect. If the plot complications have to do with ethical dilemmas, the cause and effect becomes the basis for understanding moral consequences as well. I once asked Harvard professor Amos Wilder if stories were found in every civilization. His answer stood my question on its head. He will forgive me if I only approximate his response:

> Civilizations are not found where there are no stories. That's because we learn from stories that there are consequences to our actions. Stories therefore provide the basis for moral thinking, and are a *prerequisite* for civilization.

What this means is that even from the imaginary and the fantastic, children learn important lessons about real life. This happens even when neither they nor the storyteller are aware that it is happening. A child learns courage from *Jack and the Beanstalk*, honesty from *The Boy Who Cried Wolf*, patience and humility from *Cinderella*.

Of the four engines that sustain the child's attention, *identification with characters* is clearly the most important. It's almost impossible to overestimate how central this process of identification is to the child's development. It is this capacity that allows children to try on different identities as they play out the various roles of their childhood adventures. Indeed, this is the very work of childhood—to explore, to imagine, to pretend, and in the pretending to develop larger and more encompassing identities.

The significance of identification with characters for the child's development has been explored extensively by psychoanalyst Bruno Bettelheim. As an analyst, Bettelheim was "confronted with the problem of deducing what experiences in a child's life are most suited to promote his ability to find meaning in his life."[3] His conclusion:

> Regarding this task, nothing is more important than the impact of parents and others who take care of the child; second in importance is our cultural heritage, when transmitted to the child in the right manner. When children are young, it is literature that carries such information best.[4]

In another place, Bettelheim relates this process to the complex interior structuring the child must master as part of his or her maturation processes:

> Just as his life is often bewildering to him, the child needs even more to be given the chance to understand himself in the complex world in which he must learn to cope. To be able to do this, the child must be helped to make some coherent sense out of the turmoil of his feelings. He needs ideas on how to bring his inner house into order. . . . The child finds this kind of meaning through fairy tales.[5]

More precisely, it is through the processes of literary identification that the child brings order out of the "turmoil of his feelings." On a basic level, the identification with Cinderella or Beanstalk Jack allows the child to externalize some of his or her internal tensions, and once having "gotten them out," then to deal with them as something other, rather than as a part of the self.

This process of externalizing internal tensions through identification happens to adults as well, who discover in a story the grace to move beyond some difficulty they face. Once I was conducting an adult education class at a church near the university. We had been discussing the parable of the prodigal son in Luke 15. In order to allow my listeners to enter more empathically into the story, I had set the class up in a large circle, with four chairs in the center. In the chairs I placed four volunteers, each of whom was assigned some role in the story—the father, the elder brother, the prodigal brother, and for good measure, the mother. I said that the story was taking place, not in first century Palestine, but in twentieth-century San Diego.

I interviewed each of the volunteers about what they were thinking as the prodigal prepared to leave the next morning. Then I simply stepped out of the conversation and allowed them to talk to each other. It wasn't very long before everything deteriorated into a heated argument, then an outright fight. The volunteers did masterful work getting into their roles as the characters of the story:

| | |
|---|---|
| Older Brother: | "Don't you give a rip about what dad has tried to do for you?" |
| Prodigal: | "You'll never be a man, because you're afraid to stand on your own two feet." |
| Father: | "Don't you talk to him like that!" |
| Mother: | "Leave him alone, he's only a baby." |
| Older Brother: | "He's a spoiled brat, Mom. He gets away with everything." |

So it went. After perhaps fifteen or twenty minutes, I changed the rules. Anyone in the circle could assume the role of one of the characters, simply by standing behind that character and placing his or her hands on the character's shoulders. I'll never forget what happened next. A little white-haired lady named Germane stood up and moved around behind the prodigal. She reached out and put her hands on the prodigal's shoulders and whispered something to the man who was playing the father. She whispered because she could hardly speak. Tears were streaming down her cheeks:

"I've been waiting nearly fifty years to ask you this," she said to the father. "Why didn't you just tell me that you wanted me to stay?"

Her real father could not, but the role-play father could.

He stood up, gathered her in his arms, and allowed her to weep on his shoulder. It was a profoundly tender gesture, and it brought, I believe, healing to a woman who had suffered a deep wound for nearly fifty years.

## Split Identifications Pull the Child Together Inside

Sometimes the processes of identification occur on a more complex level. The child may not identify completely with this or that character against the other characters, but rather he or she identifies partially with several characters. When this happens, the resolution of the plot complications enables the child to resolve those tensions in a healthy way.

In a comment on the story, "Sinbad the Sailor and Sinbad the Porter," Bettelheim describes the psychological dynamics by which the listening child "gets under the skin" of these two incarnations of Sinbad. Sinbad the Sailor is the swashbuckling adventurer, given to the fantastic, the life beyond the humdrum safety of the palace walls. For the sailor, *palace* means prison. Sinbad the Porter is his counterpart, overtaken with the responsibilities and burdens of reality, and afraid to venture beyond the palace walls. For the porter, *palace* means fortress, and place of security. Bettelheim remarks:

> The fairy tale helps us to understand ourselves better, as in the story the two sides of our ambivalences are isolated and projected each onto a different figure. We can visualize these ambivalences much better when the instinctual id pressures are projected onto the intrepid, immensely rich voyager who survives when all others are destroyed. . . . The opposite, reality-oriented ego tendencies are embodied in the hard-working, poor porter.[6]

More simply put, the part of the child that wants to see Tibet identifies with the sailor, while the part that wants the safety of the kitchen identifies with the porter. As the plot complicates, the conflict between the sailor and the porter raises a mirroring conflict within the child's subconscious mind. No small part of the pleasure of the listening experience lies in the conflicting emotions that that internalized dissonance can evoke. The business of identifying with characters thus forms another engine that drives the reading or listening process forward and keeps the story in flight.

We can also see the process of split identifications in the story of Wiley and his encounter with the Hairy Man, though this takes a bit of careful thought. It's easy enough to see how a child might identify with Wiley, but where does the identification with the Hairy Man take place? In the child's unruly side! We see vestiges of the magical self in the so-called Terrible Twos. A two-year-old child undergoes an almost instant demotion from being nearly godlike ("All I have to do is cry and something warm is placed in my mouth") to being absolutely the lowest person in rank anywhere in the universe ("No! Because mommy says so, that's why.") The demotion is a shock to the system, but against his or her better judgment the child learns that there are indeed limits to what one can have and where one can go and what one can say.

But what happens to the part of the child that does not want to lose that power? It does not simply go away. Rather, it has to be brought under mastery to the more acceptable self. But it stays. And that side of the self, that unruly, fierce side of the self, the side part of the self that does not want to obey, the side that does not want to wash, the side of the self that is *shaggy,* identifies with the figure of the Hairy Man. As the story progresses, the acceptable, obedient, controlled side of the self—represented by Wiley—confronts the unruly, uncontrolled self—the Hairy Man—and brings it under mastery. Indeed, this may be exactly why the children in the Sacramento airport were so fascinated with the grotesque, bizarre images of the Loathly Lady. The images of a Loathly Lady or a Hairy Man give them a safe way to revisit uncomfortable parts of themselves, and to reaffirm in their imaginations that their internalized Bogey Man will not get them in the end, that Wiley returns home to Mama safe and sound.

Bettelheim's bottom line is this: If the complication of the plot drives the listening process forward, its crisis and resolution provide the primary vehicle by which the child can "bring his inner house into order:"

> When the fairy story indicates that these two very different persons are actually "brothers under the skin," it guides the child toward the preconscious realization that these two figures are really two parts of one and the same person: that the id is as much an integral part of the our personality as the ego.[7]

The fairy story is perceived to be safe, much as the way watching a movie in a theater can be safe. I loved the suspense film *Speed* starring Sandra Bullock, but only because I knew that while my imagination was careening wildly through the city streets, my bottom was held firmly in place in the theater. Just as we might enjoy the tension in Sandra Bullock's film, so too the child may actually enjoy the psychological tension in a story. Because it is safe, the child can use the structures of the story as an environment in which to imagine and deal with fears, suspicions, and dreams of bravado. What's more, the child can do so without having to worry about real-life consequences. The most important point here is that when the resolution of the conflict in the plot becomes the source for the resolution of the conflict in the psyche, the story becomes a vehicle for wholeness and integration.[8]

The upshot of this process is that stories are a central and important resources upon which children naturally draw as they construct their understanding of the world and their place within it. Sounds, sights, sudden turns in the plot, identification with characters both good and bad—all add up to learning. In the same way they use stories to construct their external world, children also use stories to construct their internal one. When we were children, we learned from stories not only what was or wasn't, but also who we were and what we were to become.

## Children Listen to Gossip in the Same Way They Listen to Fairy Tales

There are two major reasons for this recitation of the child's processes of listening. The first is the primary thesis of this chapter: *Children listen to gossip in the same way they listen to any other story.* A child who cannot tell that water poured into a tall cylinder changes only shape, but not quantity, cannot be expected to tell that we should listen to fairy tales one way, and gossip in another. Like almost all other human transactions, this too, is a learned skill.

As children listen to the dinner table conversations they listen for sounds and visual images, they want to know what happened next and next, and they identify with the characters their parents are gossiping about. This means that when we talk about other people, our children listen as though we are talking about *them*.

Once, when my son Jonathan was eight years old, I met a cute little eight-year-old girl at church. That afternoon over dinner I mentioned her to my wife.

"I met the cutest little eight-year-old girl in church today," I said.

Jonathan interrupted me: "I'm not little and I'm not cute."

"I'm not talking about you, Jonathan. I'm talking about a girl I met in church today."

"I know that," he said, "but you said she was eight. I'm eight, and I want you to know that I'm not cute!"

As Jonathan listened to my opening sentence he began looking for some point of entry into the story so he could fill the gaps in the language. Naturally he could only do this out of his own store of knowledge and experience. The conduit from that point of entry led directly *inside* the character of the little girl, so Jonathan found himself wearing her skin and listening as though I were talking about him.

This is a strategy of listening that usually works out pretty well, especially when the child is listening to fairy stories and other well constructed children's literature. But when the child is listening to gossip, and when the gossip is malicious, the effect on the child's inner life can be disastrous. There are fundamental differences in structure and intent between literature and gossip, especially the malicious talk we normally associate with that term. Literature is generally read in a safe, neutral context. Gossip is sometimes driven by anxiety. Here we should recall the point with which we closed chapter 4:

> The perception of threat squeezes the color out of the issues and turns everything black and white, and the greater the sense of threat, the more this is likely to happen. Indeed, the degree of injustice collecting in a community's gossip is a telling indicator of its larger sense of anxiety! All of this yields a kind of guideline: *The degree of threat present appears to have an effect on the ways we interpret the events we're gossiping about. The greater our need to reduce our anxiety, the more black and white our gossip will be.*

When the dinner table talk is rounded and colorful, the child learns how to manage a complex and difficult world. When the talk is redemptive and forgiving, the child learns to be forgiving of his or her own inner life, to be accepting of the rich and varied texture of human experience. Children also learn that, should they make a major mistake, still their parents will be there for them, ready and willing to help.

By contrast, when the talk is hostile and judgmental, when it is driven by anxiety and fear, when it is malicious, it can teach the children what parts of their inner lives are forbidden territory. Literature paints its characters in color, and encourages a wide range of empathies; malicious gossip paints its characters in black and white, and asks the listener to join in the condemnation. Literature resolves its plot complications, and enables the child to resolve his or her internal psychological conflicts; malicious gossip stops its stories cold, often ending on a note of clear and outright criticism. The result is that instead of the pleasure that is evoked by the complication and resolution of plot in formal literature, malicious gossip evokes a heightened sense of danger, a moral cusp on which the child can snag his or her sense of the self.

This leads us to the second reason for this recitation of the ways children listen to stories. While literary narratives enable the resolution of inner conflict by resolving their plot complications, gossip works in a fundamentally different way and produces the opposite result: *To the extent that the child has identified with the person being talked about, he or she is left in a psychological bind, without a strategy of resolution.* The only available psychological move the child can make is to disown that portion of the self, and to identify all the more closely with the prejudiced and controlling points of view that are expressed in the gossip. People like us are never like that. We're good. Those people are bad. Any part of myself that is like that must be bad, too.

Indeed, the more black and white the gossip, the more distressing this experience is for children, although the distress may remain unconscious and therefore unvoiced. Children may find themselves troubled by the gossip, not because "those people got themselves in trouble by acting like that," but because on a preconscious level they become aware that some part of themselves is dangerous or distasteful or evil.

What are the stories told around your table and in your living room like? What sounds are used to describe someone who has done wrong? What images are evoked to discuss heaven or hell or the new principal at the high school? How are the characters developed and how are the stories resolved?

It takes very little imagination to envision the types of stories that can lead a child to disown parts of the self: Aunt Joanne had to have an abortion because she got involved with a drug dealer, how stupid can a person be? The neighbor child is writing graffiti on the garage doors again, he'll end up just like his father. The Smith boy is called into the ministry, but then he was always a good boy, his great granddaddy was a preacher in the Fire Baptized Holiness Church, why can't you be like that?

Or the child is seated beside his father in the New York subway, and he hears his father say to his mother, "If those kids were mine, I'd beat the daylights out of them!" The gossip becomes a vehicle of inner splintering. The Hairy Man hides, but he doesn't go away.

CHAPTER EIGHT

# BEHIND OUR BACKS

## When We're Spooked by Our Own Shadows

*Sometimes I get all mixed up at myself, and something inside is bugging me. Like when I say I ain't gonna do something that's no good. I do it anyway and I hate it and myself, too. So it must be something in me that's making me do it. Like when I make up my mind I won't do something bad, I do it anyway. Sometimes it seems like I can't do anything right, and there's always bad things nearby. It's like I'm two people fighting. I want to do what God wants me to do. But it's very hard.*

—Romans 7:15-17, paraphrased by Carl Burke

One of my favorite comic book characters was the Incredible Hulk, a character made famous later on a TV show of the same name, starring Bill Bixby and Lou Ferrigno. The thesis of both the comic books and the TV show was that a scientist named Dr. David[1] Banner has been exposed to an experimental drug that makes it difficult for him to control intense emotion. In moments of stress he turns into a huge, frightening, green monster—The Incredible Hulk. The unspoken premise of the story is that the "monster" is actually another side of Banner's self, a side that he struggles to control but without success. The Hulk never actually hurts anyone in either the comic books or the TV series, but still it frightens everyone, and there is a kind of manhunt in which the authorities are trying to track it down. So Banner is a man on the run, from the authorities certainly, but also from the Hulk within himself that comes out just often enough to terrorize his friends, complicate his life, and keep him always on the move.

Dr. Banner was not the only one who carried on two lives. Spiderman, another character of the Marvel comic universe, did the same. So did the characters of the DC comics—Wonder Woman and Superman. What made Banner different is that the others could choose when they would slip into their alter egos; all they needed was a phone booth or a blind alley in which to make the switch. But with Banner, the Hulk seemed to have a life of its own. In fact, Banner worked actively at keeping the Hulk down because every time it came out it left not only his clothes, but also his life, in tatters.

Why, I wonder, do these stories and the others like them hold such a fascination for us? I contend that they share the same psychological connection we traced out with Wiley and the Hairy Man in chapter 7. As the child listens to the Wiley story, an important part of the listening process is split identification, in which the child subconsciously reaffirms control over the Hairy Man within. And as we watch Banner deal again and again the Hulk within himself, we can somehow identify with his plight because we too may wrestle with parts of ourselves we do not want anyone to know about. When we do this well, those parts of the inner self can become resources for power, courage, and greater integrity. When we do it poorly we may have trouble managing the secret self, and it may explode on the scene in ways that, like the Hulk, frighten and trouble us.

This secret self is the self we disowned as we listened to our parents and other adults talk when we were children.

This disowning is especially severe for children in families where the daily gossip over the dinner table is laced with talk about black-and-white morality and absolute right and wrong. It is deepened by those overheard conversations where human acts of fear, loneliness, and despair, inherent in us all, are castigated as abnormal and shameful. When our conversations are not balanced by an equally rich vocabulary of compassion, grace, forgiveness, and redemption we are likely to infect our children with what psychologist Nathaniel Brandon calls "moral terror of the inner life."[2] Whether we are intentional about it or not, at the dinner table, in the church foyer, and on the playground, overheard conversations form—and sometimes de-form—the inner lives of our children.

## Enter the Shadow

Psychologists, pastors, and teachers regularly deal with this secret self in our work, though we deal with it in different ways. Psychiatrist Carl Jung describes his own experience of the disowned self. It occurred during a now famous dream sequence. In the dream, Jung was engulfed in fog and was being chased by a looming, dark presence behind him. He had no idea what the presence was, but he knew that it terrified him. All he had for light was a candle, which he held out in front. What was odd and frightening was that every time the candle flared up to give more light, the dark presence behind him loomed up closer and darker.

One import of the dream is that the dark presence was Jung's own "Shadow," cast behind him against the fog by the flaring of the flame. The brighter the flame, the darker and more terrifying the Shadow. Jung's work is largely based on the exploration of this "Shadow self," and the tension-ridden relationship between the Shadow and the public selves—the masks we wear to keep the Shadow hidden.

Preachers and pastoral caregivers also encounter the Shadow as a dilemma in spirituality. Sometimes it peeps out from behind the masks of the most mild-mannered and Christian faces seated in the pews in front of us as we preach. For several years my wife and I served as ministers to single adults in a large church in southern California. In time we gradually learned the private stories of the singles in our congregation. One young man had been divorced, but no one else knew it. A young woman had had an abortion when she was in her early teens. Another woman was troubled by the emotional scars left by an abusive parent. A teenager had talked of suicide, and his parents were in despair about what to do.

Many of these things we were told in confidence, and so we never repeated them to the other members of the group, even when to do so might have solved some puzzle or resolved some difficult issue in a relationship. Such is the nature of pastoral confidentiality. In time we began to realize that we were ministering not to one congregation but to two. There was the "official" public face of the congregation, in which everything was tidy, and the church looked like the ideal for which we all hoped and prayed. And then there was the church's other face, its Shadow self, peering out from behind the masks. We planned our care for the one church by holding organization meetings and watching the statistics as the group grew. But we cared for the other by listening long and hard for the things the members of our congregation were unable to say out loud.

Pastoral counselors and psychologists actively work at creating emotional safe houses in which people can deal with their Shadow selves without being judged or condemned in retaliation. As people approach moments of self-disclosure, they sometimes test us to see just how safe we will prove to be. They may disclose something not so objectionable as a way of seeing how we might react if we knew the whole truth. Presbyterian pastor Scott Dudley tells of a counseling session that took place during the hospital internship phase of his ministerial training. He was counseling with a woman whose husband had recently passed away.

"He was a good man," she said. "We're all going to miss him. Nearly a perfect man. Except for the fact that he dropped his socks on the floor sometimes. But I could deal with that."

Dudley recorded this comment, together with his response, and presented it to his supervisor for review.

"Why didn't you ask her about the socks?" asked the supervisor.

"Why should I?" said Dudley.

"She was testing you. Go back and ask about the socks."

When he did, she began to uncover a tale of unaddressed angers, brutality, and neglect. Why could she not have said that up front? Because she felt that one must honor the dead, that they have no voice to defend themselves. On another level, she could not say these things out loud because she was deathly afraid of being ground up in the rumor mill of her husband's family. Besides, she said, the whole business was now in the past. But it wasn't in the past. It was a lingering web of guilt, fear, and unhealed hurt by which her dead husband still held her hostage. She was plagued by the moral terror of the inner life, spooked by her own Shadow.

On a deeper level, because of the "moral terror of the inner life," we are sometimes afraid of our own responses to the challenges our Shadow selves bring us. How is a woman to understand who she is when she discovers that she still has unresolved anger toward her dead husband? How can she look herself in the eye? Our work among the singles in our congregation told us that such conflicts aren't at all uncommon. Sometimes the members of our congregation found aspects of their inner lives so painful that they refused to acknowledge that they were there. Our inner lives can frighten us so badly that we cannot face them at all; we too are spooked by our own Shadows.

## Repressing and Masking the Shadow

When I was a boy, something happened to me on the side yard of the house where we lived. I do not know what it was. Instead of a clear memory I have an almost palpable sense of terror. I believe that I was beaten, but I do not remember that. Every time I try and recover the memory I break down in sobs, so for now I am preparing for a visit that I know I will someday be able to make. A psychologist would say that that memory is *repressed.*

Suppose that a happily married businessman finds himself physically attracted to his secretary. Not wanting to allow the attraction to get the upper hand, he develops a strategy of being curt with her whenever they are alone. His curtness is a way of disguising the attraction, and it may work so well that it disguises the attraction even from the businessman himself! But the attraction is still there, driving his bad manners. In this case, we would say that the businessman has *masked* the attraction. The grand things Scott Dudley's patient said about her dead husband are yet another way of masking. Those things that we must mask or repress provide clues about important dimensions of our spirituality.

Almost all of us have worked or worshiped with people who have masked or repressed issues that are visible to everybody else, but that they themselves cannot see. When we are unable to face our Shadows they can exert extraordinary control over us even without our knowledge. Repressed parts of the self do not go away. Instead, they just cook beneath the surface like volcanoes, and when the pressure gets to be too great they explode. That's why we sometimes find people changing into real hulks, right before our eyes.

## Keith

Once a student named Keith told me point-blank through gritted teeth that he could kill his father. I absolutely believed him. It happened like this: Keith had failed a freshman religion course, and then had taken it again to correct the grade on his transcript. This second time through, he showed up thirty minutes late for the final exam. I told him he could take the exam, but that I would like to see him in private when he was finished. We stepped out into the hall.

"Keith," I said. "You're going to have to take charge of your own education. This is like going to the gym. Nobody can do it for you. You have to do it for yourself."

That was all I said to him. It took perhaps thirty seconds. In that time he became explosive. Like a real-life David Banner, he transformed into an Incredible Hulk. He stared straight ahead at a place perhaps four or five inches in front of his face. His back became ramrod rigid, and his jaw clenched. At the same time he began clenching his fists and shaking all over. He was a big kid who had been a football player in high school, but I had a sense that he was stretching himself out the way Wiley did in the presence of the Hairy Man. He almost loomed over me.

I could tell that he had been thrown suddenly into a terrible psychological crisis so I changed the direction of my comments. "Keith," I said, "I'm going to ask you something. You don't have to answer me because I don't have any right to know this. Did your father beat you when you were little?"

"It's in my past," he said, through his clenched teeth. The clenching of his jaw made his response sound like a growl.

"No, it's not," I said. "It's in your present. If you don't deal with this, it's in your future, too."

"No, it's not," he said. "Because I know I can kill him if I need to." These last words he spat at me.

As we talked, Keith calmed down enough to tell me some of his story. Before we finished I referred him to a counselor who could help him deal with the psychological wounds that his father had left. As a theologian and pastoral caregiver I continued to be concerned with the spiritual and theological dimensions of this problem that I knew would radically affect his spiritual life.

First, I knew that because Keith had grown up in the shadow of a rigid and vindictive father he would be likely to see God in the same light. The tendency to form our earliest and most enduring impressions of God on the basis of our experiences of our fathers is well documented. In Keith's case this tendency was worsened by the fact that his father was an ordained minister. Keith's impressions of God were formed not only by the violence his father had inflicted on him—to a child, surely a foregrounding of hell—but also by the rigid black and white of his father's graceless perfectionism. Whatever he may have said from his pulpit, in his actions and his talk Keith's father demonstrated a religious life in which God was both graceless and violent. The struggle between Keith's inner and outer selves would be among the most challenging and troubling aspects of his journey toward spiritual maturity and wholeness.

Second, Keith's repressed anger absorbed enormous amounts of emotional and psychological energy. The next time I saw him, he apologized to me for his outburst about killing his father. "I wasn't myself," he said. But he was wrong. The *self* that is Keith is a self that contains within it a smoldering volcano of anger. Let's explore this metaphor for a moment. Scientists who study volcanoes regularly comment on the extraordinary destructive forces that are unleashed in an eruption—tons of hot air and ashes, followed by a mountain of molten magma, sometimes several thousand degrees in heat, traveling at thirty to forty miles an hour. But think about how much energy is expended keeping all that force in place as the volcano builds toward eruption! This was something like what happened within Keith, too. The energy he spent when he exploded at me was an indicator of the amount of energy he was spending every minute of every day keeping his seething anger repressed.

Repression and masking are equal opportunity destroyers. This is like holding a soccer ball under water. Unless we are extraordinarily strong, or extraordinarily determined, sooner or later the ball will win. In a major study of publicly stigmatized people, social scientist Erving Goffman describes the personal costs of living behind a mask.[3] Imagine, says Goffman, that you are an African-American with fair skin and enough Anglo features that you could "pass" in white society. For whatever reason, that is the choice you make. What does that choice cost you? It means that whatever you do, and wherever you go, you will have to be on your guard against discovery. You will have to filter every story you tell, every conversation, every contact, for clues that might give you away. If people love and admire you, you alone know that their love and admiration is based on a fiction. The most terrible price you pay is that you can never go home. You are cut off from your roots, from the deepest sources of who you are. Your self is reduced to the roles you play. You become a kind of David Banner, on the run to protect the Hulk from discovery. The amount of energy involved in that process is enormous.

This, then, is the third problem with Keith's keep-a-cork-on-it way of dealing with his inner life: The struggle not to feel anger demands so much internal energy that it smothers out the other emotions as well. As psychologists Connie Zweig and Stephen Wolfe have said, in the operating room the anesthesia prevents one from feeling pain, but also prevents one from feeling joy.

The fourth, and in some ways the saddest thing about Keith's way of dealing with his Shadow self is that he had every right to be angry at his father. His father had taken from him something precious and important. The problem wasn't that Keith was angry, but that he didn't know how to manage his anger in productive ways.

He did not tell me this, but I think I can guess what happened to make his anger such a problem for him. One of the ways I expressed care for Keith was that I wrote him a story about a young boy who wakes up in the night and discovers a dragon in his father's bed. In time the dragon becomes violent and the boy is almost killed in a massive battle of wills between the dragon and himself. Eventually, he wins this battle and the dragon is destroyed, but an old man cautions the boy: "Be careful, because you may have given birth to the same dragon within yourself." The boy is thrown into a situation of anguish, because this was the one thing about his father he most despised.

I believe that this is what happened with Keith. When his father became angry and then violent, Keith promised himself that he would never turn out like that. The anger within himself was a very real part of who he was, but it was something in his inner life that terrified him. In his view, anger itself was a hateful thing, something one should stuff into the Shadow. Keith believed that if he ever got angry, the result would be catastrophic, so—like David Banner—he kept on the run and tried to stay away from stressful situations. When anger erupted, he told himself, "I'm sorry, I wasn't myself." But the anguish remained. In this way, Keith was cheated of an essential note of his emotional repertoire. He needs to have the ability to feel anger if he is ever going to be whole.

Keith's story was the David Banner story, and the story of Dr. Jekyl and Mr. Hyde. It is my contention that Keith's story is also the story of all those quiet, unassuming members of our singles congregation who struggled—sometimes heroically—to deal with parts of themselves they did not really know how to handle. It's also my story. The differences in our difficulties are not differences of *kind*, but only of *degree*. Many of us escaped the kind of violence Keith experienced, but we didn't escape the subtle pervasive effect of the gossip. Those effects were tiny and incremental, but like the effects of children's literature, they were cumulative over time. As we listened to the talk we learned in a thousand ways that there were parts of ourselves—pint-sized Hulks perhaps—that were not welcome here. The result is that we have all developed public selves that we protect at all costs, and then struggle with Shadow selves that sometimes frighten and confuse us.

### The Shadow and the Spiritual Journey

The war between the public and the private selves is the source of a great deal of confusion about the nature of the spiritual life, and—like the gossip that creates it—it significantly impacts the ways we come to terms with the other obstacles and challenges we encounter along the road. Just as Keith is likely to develop an image of a harsh and vindictive God, many ordinary Christians struggle in the night with an image of a God who speaks with the voice of their disgruntled fathers: "If those children were mine I'd beat the daylights out of them."

Just as Keith repressed his anger until it erupted like Vesuvius, so did the quieter, more controlled members of my congregation manifest their Shadow selves in shame, in deeply seated perfectionism, in harsh judgmentalism, in an inability to tolerate differences of opinion, in unhealthy self-sacrifice, in an inability to forgive those who have hurt them, or in bailing out on the church before they were found out. Just as Keith would have to deal in time with the raw edge of tension between his inner and his outer lives, so also do the rest of us. The struggle between our inner and our outer selves is among the most challenging and troubling aspects of our journey to spiritual maturity and wholeness.

Yet this is also one of the things we talk about least in our spiritual retreats, Bible studies, and workshops. We do not talk about it because talk about a troubled inner life is taboo in the church; it violates our hermeneutic of everyday life; it fills us with a sense of shame. And yet, ironically—as we saw in chapter 3—*talking* about life is our primary way of coming to understand it. It's terribly difficult to deal with the Shadow when we cannot even say aloud that we have one, let alone look it square in the eye!

In chapters 9, 10, and 11, I will explore some of the specific ways Christians have dealt with this problem, including some of the ways Christian theology and practice can make it worse, and some of the unique and distinctive ways the faithful and redemptive talk in the Christian community, the frank recognition of our common humanity, and the living reality of grace can bring it to healing. For now it is enough to point out that much of what passes for spiritual discipline or maturity—much of what passes for *religion*—is in reality a struggle to keep the Hulks within ourselves from breaking out and making a mess of our outer lives.

CHAPTER NINE

# SCAPEGOATING KENNETH

## Good Kids, Bad Kids, and Cootie Girls

*Most of us, most of the time, feel left out—misfits. We don't belong. Others seem to be so confident, so sure of themselves, "insiders" who know the ropes, old hands in a club from which we are excluded.*

*The terrible price we pay for keeping all those other people out so that we can savor the sweetness of being insiders is a reduction of reality, a shrinkage of life. Nowhere is this price more terrible than when it is paid in the cause of religion.*

—Eugene Petersen

Ann-Marie was almost a stereotype. She was bright but not brilliant, a good student, but driven to her studies by something inside her, rather than drawn in by the material she was studying. What mattered to her was not the subject matter, but the grades. Ann-Marie was going for the golden ring. I knew she was in trouble when she came to me in despair after receiving a "B" on a major research paper. A "B" is a respectable grade, an indication of solid, responsible work, but Ann-Marie was devastated.

I asked her to join me in the faculty dining room, where we found a quiet corner and explored together the root causes of her discouragement. As her teacher and caregiver, I sensed that a good place to start would be to map the territory of her family relationships. The first thing that stood out to me was that her grandfather was a famous theologian, with a long list of publications and a wide reputation as a preacher in the northwest. Her father had not gone into the ministry, and had instead chosen a career in banking and investment, much to the disappointment of her grandparents. Ann-Marie's sister had married right out of high school and was now a single mother, raising two young children. Her brother Kenneth had abandoned the faith altogether, and—as Ann-Marie said it—he had "gone bad." He used drugs and had gotten his high school girlfriend pregnant. He was occasionally in trouble with the law. She volunteered the information about Kenneth, but I could have guessed as much. A significant number of my most dedicated theology students have a sibling somewhere who epitomizes everything they themselves would not want—or dare!—to be. Kenneth was the second thing that stood out to me as we talked.

In contrast, Ann-Marie was the family's golden girl. Of the three children, she was the only one to go to college. That was the third thing that stood out.

"I have to do well," she said. "I can't fail. My parents are depending on me." The depth of her parents' dependence upon her was marked out in the panic in her eyes.

We talked about her sense of panic. Was it her own, or was it theirs? This was only a step. It was not enough to map the terrain of her family life, for two reasons. First, what shapes us is not only what happens to us, but also our *interpretation* of what happens to us, as well as the choices we ourselves make by way of response, and the things we say to everyone else and to ourselves to validate our position. Second, if we cannot talk about something, we have a harder time understanding it. Yet the parts of the family life that matter most are often the parts no one talks about because they're smothered in a blanket of taboo. Beneath the carefully manicured landscapes of our family histories there are hidden faults and fissures, areas of conviction as solid as granite, and molten areas seething toward eruption. There are also the enormous forces of avoidance. In the words of an adult child of an alcoholic, "In my family there were two very clear rules: the first was that there is nothing wrong here, and the second was, don't tell anyone."[1] The strategies of avoidance are the fourth thing that stood out to me as Ann-Marie and I talked.

These things are the compass points of Ann-Marie's inner life, her primary way of orienting herself within her private world. She knew who she was in response to these—her family's unspoken expectations and deepest disappointments, their angers, their hopes, their shattered dreams, their unhealed wounds, and their unspoken and unforgiven guilt. In a sense, Ann-Marie was her parents' last and best hope of turning out to be adequate as parents. She accepted this role the way an athlete goes into training, with discipline and energy. Her father and mother were coach and cheer squad, always there on the sidelines. They had a lot at stake in Ann-Marie's success—she was also her father's last, best chance of fulfilling grandpa's legacy, stepping into his giant shoes.

I have told this story in some detail, but it's not really about Ann-Marie. It's about her brother Kenneth. What happened to Ann-Marie had happened to her brother in reverse. In the same way that Ann-Marie bore the weight of her parents' unrealized dreams, Kenneth bore their disappointments and their sense of inadequacy as parents.

Kenneth was the family scapegoat.

## Scapegoats and Cootie Girls

Scapegoating is perhaps the most ugly combination of our worst fears, our Shadow selves, expressed in our gossip and eventually our actions. The term "scapegoat" comes to us from the Old Testament, where it refers to an annual ritual by which the sins of the people were ceremonially transferred to a goat. Acting in the role of priest, Aaron was instructed to lay his hands upon the head of the scapegoat, and there to make his corporate confession of guilt. The goat was then driven out into the desert where it was left to perish (Leviticus 16:20-28). The scapegoat served not only a ritual function, but also a psychological one: It allowed the community to envision itself now redeemed and purified of those sins that had troubled its deepest consciousness. In the terms we are developing in this book, the scapegoat was a public, ritualized way of managing the community's Shadow self.

What do we do with the Shadow self when there is no longer an Aaronic priest or a literal goat? In chapter 4, I said that gossip is a primary means of reducing anxiety and managing power. When the source of the anxiety is *outside* of us, we can triangle our friends, but what do we do if the anxiety comes from within us? What do we do if, like Dr. David Banner, we carry within ourselves an Incredible Hulk lurking in the wings to make his desperate appearance? What does Kenneth's father do with his sense of shame at his failure to live up to his own father's legacy?

Scapegoating is a common way of dealing with such things. When we scapegoat we project on someone else those things we find most troubling about ourselves, then we hate them there. Thus, we force a human player into that role, symbolically requiring him or her to bear the sin, the guilt, and the shame we cannot face within ourselves.

Human scapegoats are a common theme in literature and storytelling. Perhaps most vivid are the nineteen victims of the Salem witchcraft trials whose story was immortalized in Arthur Miller's chilling play, *The Crucible*. In the introductory pages of the play, Miller points out that the sins of which the Salem witches were accused were in reality those of the accusers:

> The witch-hunt was not, however, a mere repression. It was also, and as importantly, a long overdue opportunity for everyone so inclined to express publicly his guilt and sins, under the cover of accusations against the victims. It suddenly became possible—and patriotic and holy—for a man to say that Martha Corey had come into his bedroom at night, and that, while his wife was sleeping at his side, Martha laid herself down on his chest and "nearly suffocated him." Of course, it was her spirit only, but his satisfaction at confessing himself was no lighter than if it had been Martha herself. One could not ordinarily speak such things in public.
>
> Long-held hatreds of neighbors could now be openly expressed, and vengeance taken, despite the Bible's charitable injunctions. Land-lust which had been expressed before by constant bickering over boundaries and deeds, could now be elevated to the arena of morality; one could cry witch against one's neighbor and feel perfectly justified in the bargain.[2]

To translate Miller's language into the terms we are developing in this book, their Shadow selves finally found an officially acceptable outlet. It's worth noting that each person accuses the witch of the very sins he himself has most rigorously repressed.

The character of Hester Prynne in Nathaniel Hawthorne's novel *The Scarlet Letter* is another example from the puritan town of Salem. In this dangerous and frightening land, the village fathers are determined to maintain a rigorous biblical discipline over the colonists in their charge. When Hester Prynne, whose husband has not yet come from England, turns up pregnant she becomes the village scapegoat. All of the villagers' repressed angers, their repressed independence, their repressed sexuality, are projected onto her, and the town lynches her—not literally, but figuratively—by forcing her to wear a scarlet letter "A" on the bodice of her dress. It is *their* Shadows that have been forced out into the open, not hers. The letter on her dress represents a target for the repressed faults and flaws, and the anxieties and shames that go with them that they subconsciously hate or fear most within themselves.

That is why the issues here do not have so much to do with Hester Prynne's act of adultery, but with the manner in which the town fathers respond to that act. In some interpretations, Hester Prynne is the prototype of the strong-minded woman, whose independence and freedom of movement make her the focus of the village rumor mill long before she becomes involved with the Reverend Arthur Dimmesdale. (Indeed, were it up to the gossips she would have been branded with a hot iron!) In the end, it is her defiant independence that brings about her ruin, and then, finally, her redemption. In the same way that Lieutenant John J. Dunbar is slated for execution at Fort Hayes, Hester Prynne is set up as an example, and therefore (not coincidentally) as a means of social control. The actions of the town fathers center around the public implications should her sin be ignored.

It's perhaps easier to identify scapegoats in literature because of the refinement of focus and emphasis that reading and writing make possible. In both *The Crucible* and *The Scarlet Letter* the townspeople are flatly developed, so that the reader has little basis of sympathy for them and can see no positive intentions in what they do. It's different in the densely textured experience of real life. The details of an event are intermixed with all sorts of other, unrelated factors, and people act out the worst sorts of evil under the guise of good intentions, even the quest for justice. In real life, recognizing scapegoats can be both more complex and more subtle.

In a contemporary retelling of the theme of the scapegoat, recording artist Michael Kelly Blanchard tells about a chance meeting with a girl from his childhood neighborhood:

I looked up at the cashier,
And there behind the rouge,
The scars and dents of a past offense
Bent me like a bruise.
As she brushed off my embarrassment
Like an actress shifting roles
I made a stab at a complement,
Then hurried out the door.

Long ago, oh I don't know,
Maybe not so long I guess
Seems she was the victim of
Our childhood thoughtlessness.
The one at times for whom taunts and rhymes
Like cruel stones were hurled.
The friendless child we all defiled,
Known as the cootie girl.

On the battlefield of the bus stop
We warriors took sides
With lethal stares we combed our hair
And primed pubescent pride.
Until the war would call a truce
When she came into view.
A common target we could shoot,
Where neither side would lose.[3]

Whenever a gang of bullies picks on a younger, smaller, or gentler child, that child is a scapegoat. Whenever an employee is fired to cover for the ineptness or dishonesties of a supervisor, that employee is a scapegoat.

## Scapegoats and Golden Girls

Very often the operative function in scapegoating is projection, which allows us to distance ourselves from our guilt by assigning that guilt to someone else. This is what happened to Kenneth. Kenneth's disappointment to his father was borne of the father's disappointment to the grandfather. If the Bible says, "the sins of the fathers are visited upon the children," it might have said just as well, "the Shadow selves of the fathers are visited upon the children."

Ann-Marie's experience was related, but opposite. She was not the family scapegoat, but she was instead a kind of sacrificial lamb. Her whole bearing shuddered under the weight of the burden she carried. The panic in her eyes was palpable. Ann-Marie's burden is a common problem for the children and grandchildren of influential people, but with a subtle, bittersweet twist. When the child is forced to serve as the family scapegoat or its sacrificial lamb, the saying, "he lived in the shadow of his father" carries a sinister and immoral subtext.

What has this to do with our subject of gossip? We can respond to this question by turning it on its head. How did Ann-Marie take upon herself the burden of her parents' successes? How did she learn that this was her role? By the same token, how did Kenneth come to be the family black sheep? More precisely, how do scapegoats become scapegoats?

Let's begin with the basic observation that Kenneth, for whatever reason, could not or would not match the expectations of his parents. Kenneth acted out. His parents, in a well-intentioned attempt to bring him back into line, disciplined him for his behavior, driving home the point with guilt trips and ridicule. More than once, they confronted him with the better example that was being set for him by his poster-child sister, Ann-Marie.

Ann-Marie overheard all of this and more. The message that she had to be the poster-child was embedded in the comments her parents made to or about her brother. Every time she heard, "Why can't you be like your sister?" she shuddered behind her mask, polished her halo, and carefully drew in any exposed corners of her Shadow self. She was listening to the talk the way children listen to Wiley and the

Hairy Man: On a deep and subconscious level she secretly identified with her brother. In doing so, she learned that the exact traits that were being condemned in him were the ones she herself must never show. Mom and Dad triangle Kenneth out on one side—the designated black sheep—and they triangle Ann-Marie in on the other side—the designated poster-child.

The more subtle and powerful reality behind this triangle is that the difficulties with Kenneth keep Ann-Marie in place. She is a *better* poster kid because her brother "went bad." There is an intimate connection between the abysmal depth of Kenneth's failures and the dazzling height of his sister's success. The connection isn't a balancing act, exactly. It's more like one of those trapeze acts in the circus, in which one gymnast leaps on the catapult, tossing the other to the high wire. Ann-Marie wears her parents' halo *because* Kenneth wears their Shadow. Had her parents been less condemning of Kenneth, she would have been less driven to do well. And that was the source of her desperation—her terror of "turning out like him." As it was, her drive to succeed was not unlike the quiet desperation felt by the children of alcoholics, who clean up their parents and run their homes and take upon themselves the thankless chore of making everything work.

I wonder how many parents would *consciously* be willing to trade off the soul of one of their children, if in the bargain they would be able to turn another into a star. In the novel *Sophie's Choice*, the main character, Sophie, is a Polish resistance fighter during World War II. She is arrested by the Gestapo and taken with her two children to the extermination facility at Birkenau. Eventually she comes to the ramp where a Nazi doctor will decide their fate. The doctor is drunk and unkempt, and he lingers with Sophie for a moment, obviously enjoying toying with her. She is Aryan, not Jewish, and she speaks flawless German. When the doctor discovers that she is a Christian, he allows her to save one of her children, but this means of course that he also forces her to decide which to send to the gas chamber.

> Her thought processes dwindled, ceased. Then she felt her legs crumple. "I can't choose! I can't choose!" . . . "Don't make me choose," she heard herself plead in a whisper. "I can't choose."
>
> "Send them both over there, then," said the doctor to the aide, "*nach links.*" *[To the left—and thus to the gas chamber.]*

What happens next is the core crisis of the novel, the horrifying vortex around which all of its psychological nuances swirl.

> "Take the baby!" she called out. "Take my little girl."[4]

The point of the book is not to explore the moral evil of the choice Sophie was forced to make, but rather the psychological and spiritual consequences within Sophie herself. As I read I couldn't help but wonder about the consequences for Joseph, the older child who survived. Will Joseph not bear an enormous psychological burden of undeserved guilt?

As Ann-Marie and I talked, the image that came to mind was the horrible actual death of one of the accused witches at Salem. On September 19, 1692, Giles Corey (who incidentally refused to confess his guilt as a witch) was placed under a wooden slab and crushed as the members of the community placed heavy stones on the slab. He literally bore the weight of the sins of the community upon himself.

That was what I saw in Ann-Marie. The weary, panicky look in her eyes told me that she, too, had been asked to bear such a weight. Only for Ann-Marie, the weight was placed there so slowly that no one noticed at the time, cumulatively, a pebble here, a grain there, an overheard guilt trip here, a cutting remark there. The stones included not only the implied message embedded in her parents' gossip—"better not fail, or you'll end up no good, just like your brother!"—but also the unacknowledged burden of her own role in her brother's failures.

Sometimes a scapegoat can hover on the borders of a community for years without being expelled, but nevertheless be forced to carry the projected failures of the community as a whole. That's because scapegoats play an important role in the social structure; they keep the existing power structure in place. It isn't just that someone gets ousted, it's that somebody gets to decide who gets ousted, and why. Scapegoating somebody is a way of showing that you have clout. The point isn't really what the powerful choose to do, but that, in choosing, they demonstrate that the authority belongs to *them*. Scapegoats also focus the group's sense of right and wrong, and in that way reinforce the boundaries between them and *us*. In that way, the group may maintain its social structures at the scapegoat's expense. In return, the members of the group can sense that they are themselves somehow *better*; and in that way they can feel a heightened sense of inclusion.

And, of course, as discussed in chapter 2, deciding who is in and who is out, who has power and who does not, what is wrong and what is right—all this is determined by our *talk*. Thus, talk is also the primary mechanism by which scapegoating takes place. Just as the gossip intensifies and becomes more black and white as the group feels itself under pressure, so also the frequency and intensity of scapegoating increases when the group feels itself to be under threat. It's not that these two social activities, gossip and scapegoating, play parallel roles, but that they play interdependent roles. Scapegoating is the effect, and gossip is the means to that effect. The church youth group can scapegoat the kid who doesn't dress according to code. The university faculty can scapegoat the professor with the unconventional opinion. Because scapegoating is a social activity, entire groups can scapegoat entire other groups, and in the same ways. The Germans scapegoated the Jews, American cowboys scapegoated Native Americans, whites scapegoat blacks, and blacks scapegoat whites.

## Scapegoating in the Name of God

Because the church is primarily an oral place, and because religion deals continually with judgments about right and wrong, it's nearly inevitable that the dynamic of scapegoating would also be part of church life. In the church, though, it can come packaged in the language of religion. We see it in the intensity with which liberal gossip demonizes fundamentalists, an intensity that may indicate that more is going on than simply sorting out who disagrees with whom. Of course, this can be said just as well in reverse: When fundamentalists talk about liberals there are no shades of gray. The very intensity of the language can be just as rigid and narrow as liberal attitudes toward fundamentalists.

Scapegoating in support of religious values and ideals can have an especially sharp edge on it because those ideals are often more perfectionistic and therefore harder to live up to. Scapegoating outsiders is a way insiders can buttress their defenses against the possibility of their own failures.

I would push the envelope further at this point. It may be that the hostile edge one finds in fundamentalist talk about liberal ideas masks or represses a deeper yearning for freedom and open-ended thought. After all, we sometimes yearn for that which also frightens us because it may be a part of our disowned selves, a part of our shadow. Conversely, the hostility the liberal directs toward the fundamentalist may mask a deeper hunger for order and responsibility within structure. The suspicions church leaders sometimes seem to have toward academics may well mask their own deep, unfulfilled dreams of free and unencumbered research, while the suspicions scholars sometimes have of church leaders may mask their own sense of loss over the immediacy and drama of ministry in the trenches. It would be an interesting exploration to see how or why Baptists scapegoat Catholics, or Pentecostals scapegoat Baptists. Whatever its form, though, the projection involved is clear.

As with conversation generally, the sanctions against those who violate religious norms can run from the extremely subtle—raised eyebrows, shifts of the eye, silence—to the extremely violent. In our more civil time, religious gossip is sometimes told in such a way that outsiders are flattened out, and the richly textured tapestry of human experience is reduced to a black-and-white photograph of insiders and outsiders. We would do well to remember that we are not very far removed from the witch trials at Salem. We are not far removed from a time in which religious sanctions against wrongdoers ran to shunning, excommunication, and hanging or burning at the stake. Our tradition of faith includes verbal dueling in which sometimes real blood is spilled!

In the stories of this chapter, I have hoped to lay bare the social and psychological impulses by which overheard gossip can lead to scapegoating, and from that to ethnic or religious prejudice. These consequences are unintended, but are nevertheless real and troubling. Issues can be traced in such stories that occupied our attention in chapter 2—the establishment of group boundaries, the establishment of points of privilege, and the exercise of power. These stories show how central *talk* is in this dynamic, and how the flow of talk can consolidate power, often at someone else's expense.

What is important here is not that the talk takes place, but that the *function* of the talk, with all of its projections and defenses, may be a way of managing parts of ourselves that we cannot face.

### By Way of Postscript

I have changed the names of Ann-Marie and Kenneth, and have modified important features of their story so that in a real sense they're something of a fiction now, no longer an exact correlation with the real human beings on whom they are based. Is this example fictional? As I've shared this chapter with colleagues and friends, many have told me that with only minor changes the dynamic of this family is the dynamic of their own.

One of my colleagues has been gracious enough to listen and comment as I read aloud. When we finished reading this chapter she made a curious and haunting remark: "If my brother ever becomes a fully functional human being, I won't know who I am." Then, after a moment's pause, she asked me this: "What do you say to Ann-Marie's parents? And what do you say to those of us who, like Ann-Marie, have come to wear our parents' halo?"

My shoot-from-the-hip response was this: What need have we for a scapegoat, when God himself has provided already a lamb for the sacrifice?

As I've thought about that response, I've come to see that I was answering a question she hadn't asked. What she was interested in was the source of forgiveness, not from God, but from her brother. Where does one find the words that can make a fresh start? Where does one find the grace to forgive? The answer to that, I believe, lies in the recognition that all of us—parents, scapegoated children, golden girls and failures, saints and sinners—stand in need of the grace that comes from the sacrifice that God has made. God has already provided a sacrificial lamb to cover all of those failings we hoped to cover on our own with a scapegoat of our own choosing. If the ground at the foot of the cross is level ground, it is ground that invites us to stand beside those children we have hurt and say with them—invites us to say *to* them—"be merciful to me, for I am a sinner."

My comment to Ann-Marie would run differently. Let us

suppose for a moment that there were two women, one seventeen years old, the other thirty-five. The seventeen-year-old finds herself one night in a bar by mistake, where she is hit on by a drunken older man. Suppose she says to the man, "No. That would be wrong. What if my mother finds out?" That would be a right response, for a perfectly adequate reason.

By chance the thirty-five-year old also finds herself in a bar, also hit upon by a drunken older man. And suppose that she, too, responds the way her younger counterpart did: "No. That would be wrong. What if my mother finds out?" That would be a right response, but for an inadequate and illegitimate reason. Something else must take place for her to function appropriately for her age. She must set down the burden of her mother's shame, and must recognize that she is herself responsible, as an adult, for whatever decision she makes at a moment like that.

Suppose that in the same way, a youngster like Ann-Marie becomes a theology student, not because she is drawn in by the material, or because she passionately loves the Lord or feels called to the vocation of ministry, but only because she is afraid that, if she chooses some other path, she would turn out like her brother and be a failure as a human being. Would that not be in its own way a choice made for an inadequate and illegitimate reason?

To Ann-Marie, then, I offer this secondary reassurance: God has provided already a lamb for the sacrifice, and has no need for you or any of us to play that role. And if God has no need for us to do this, then we are released at last to set down the heavy burden of our parents' halo and choose some other path—or to choose this one—as the leading of our own hearts require.

CHAPTER 10

# MORAL TERROR OF THE INNER LIFE

## The Four Horsemen of the Inner Apocalypse

*Beware of the yeast of the Pharisees, that is, their hypocrisy. Nothing is covered up that will not be uncovered, and nothing secret that will not become known. Therefore whatever you have said in the dark will be heard in the light, and what you have whispered behind closed doors will be proclaimed from the housetops.*

—Luke 12:1-3

*We seem willing enough to claim the connection between "the American Dream" and the enterprising, pragmatic kind of people we are, but we disown the connection between the Shadow side of our society and the kind of people we are. Each of us tries to hide our inner "trash": our violence, our mortality, the poverty of our inadequacy. If it does sometimes seem easy to fool ourselves in this way, Jesus' words come to us as a fresh caution.*

—Elaine Prevallet
Commenting on Luke 12:1-3

As I discussed the contents of this book with friends and colleagues, one of them offered a striking illustration. She had come to our luncheon with the fresh memory of the funeral of one of the members of her congregation who had only the week before committed suicide. We'll call him Karl, though she never mentioned his name. Karl's death was sudden, completely unexpected. No one in the congregation or the pastoral staff knew that he was in despair. He was middle-aged and single, an active member of the church's adult education program. To all outward appearances he was content with his life, a quiet man, and apparently cheerful. After his suicide, his family discovered among his things a journal that was riddled with comments about his struggle with a secret, deeply seated homosexual tendency.

"It was easier for him to kill himself than it was to risk the consequences of exposure among the people he knew and loved," my pastor friend told me. In the quiet moments that followed this comment, we shared together our amazement at the extraordinary steps we will take to keep our Shadows in the shadows.

Throughout this book I have explored instances of people in personal and relational difficulties that are connected in various ways with their Shadow selves or the Shadow selves of those who were responsible for their care, and how gossip can either suppress or coax out the Shadow. In chapter 4, we explored John's problems with the campaign of gossip that was generated against him by the organist at his church, and in chapter 5, Lori's deep sense of having been left exposed by my story of the princess who lived in a prison. There was the matter of Keith's smoldering anger that occupied our attention in chapter 8, and the scapegoating of Kenneth, and the consequences for Ann-Marie we discussed in chapter 9.

These are all problems of profound depth, if only because they seem to hold their victims in suspended states of crisis, like being caught in real-life human spiderwebs, unable to move. In every single instance, the problems of the Shadow were made worse by the steps these people were taking to protect their Shadows from discovery. What I have pointed out here is that these are also problems of profound crisis for the *spiritual* lives of all of these people. Virtually all of the stories we have discussed in this book are about deeply committed religious people—people of faith. Yet every one would tell you that getting untangled from the web is harder than it looks, that it's something different from confessing one's sins or "claiming the promises of God," and that "getting one's theology right" doesn't really seem to help, either. Like my friend's parishioner Karl, sometimes it seems like it must be easier to take one's life than it is to share that life with the people who mean the most to us.

Why is it so hard? In a sense, the problem Karl felt was not so much the Shadow self, but the fear of exposure. He had managed to hide his homosexuality from his family and friends, and so far as we know had functioned quite well without ever acting out this tendency. What troubled him was not the homosexuality itself, but the underlying sense of being somehow defective, with the self-contempt that goes with that feeling. The fear of exposure also played a large role. He couldn't bear the agony of being found out. He had heard enough talk about homosexuality growing up to know what people would think about him. The glue that held him stuck in the web was the belief that there was something about himself that everyone he knew and loved would find foreign and unlovable.

We have a tiny inkling of what desperate fear of exposure must be like when we find ourselves in one of those crazy-making conversations in which the people we're talking with are trashing someone who isn't present. We ourselves become embarrassed—"If they knew the truth about me, they would be talking this same trash to someone else—

*about me.*" Psychologists and pastoral caregivers group those feelings together under the term, *shame.*

In a now famous study entitled *Shame: The Power of Caring*, psychiatrist Gershen Kaufman identifies four different common reactions to the feelings of shame that are associated with the Shadow, though he does not use Jung's term.[1] According to Kaufman, the four primary "defenses against shame" are these: rage, withdrawal, perfectionism, and the abuse of power. I call these the four horsemen of the inner apocalypse, the riders whose appearance can signal impending disaster. In those very responses, the Shadow shows not only its presence but also its extraordinary power. While the four horsemen try hard to keep the Shadow hidden, ironically they do the opposite. The perceptive observer will see them as symptoms of the Shadow; very often they telegraph the presence of the very thing they're trying to disguise! Our boss denies our request for a raise, and we yell at our children. Our business plan goes sour and our sense of competence is in jeopardy, and we withdraw into drink. Psychologists sometimes say that in these responses the Shadow is "slipping out sideways," showing itself in the very efforts we make to keep it hidden.

## The Horseman of Rage

Of the four horsemen of the inner apocalypse, perhaps the most immediately identifiable is rage. It works as a kind of defense because it distances the person who has shamed us. This is what David and Lori expected to happen when they appeared at my office door that morning to confront me with having humiliated Lori. David would growl at me, there would be intense eye contact, I would cower, and perhaps beg her forgiveness. In the event that I didn't do that, he would beat me up, and they could still leave angry, but self-righteous. When instead I invited them in and listened carefully to their complaint, they were surprised, and their rage deflected. We went on from that experience to become good friends; the following year I even wrote David a letter of recommendation to graduate school.

As we saw in chapter 9, one strategy for dealing with the Shadow self is projection. I repress some troubling aspect of my inner life by projecting it on someone else, then hating it there. What this means is that projection coupled with rage is a form of self-hatred. But of course, I may use rage in its more common forms as a way of defending against exposure as well.

We also saw rage in the story of my student Keith, who told me he could kill his father. The anger he felt, the gritted teeth, the stiffening in his back, the growling remark that he could kill the man, all indicated his struggle to manage something that was seething deep within himself. Keith's rage was more urgent and more impulsive than David's, a deep inner cauldron of anger already boiling over. His rage wasn't particularly directed at me, but every movement, every gesture signaled me to watch out, that something dangerous was brewing here. The rage was directed instead at Keith's father—or perhaps the internalized voice of his father. He had learned from his father this way of muscling his inner life back under control.

How tragically like his father he was, and how agonizing his struggle to keep everything under wraps. But there's a kernel of hope here. If Keith learns to recognize that parallel, if he comes to terms with his own struggle with rage, he may find in that discovery the beginning steps he needs to take if he is ever going to understand and forgive his father.

## The Horseman of Withdrawal

The second horseman of the inner apocalypse is withdrawal. One hot afternoon I raised the issue of the Shadow self in a course about religious experience and contemporary personal issues. As I described the Shadow and the things we do to avoid exposure, the students underwent a gradual, barely perceptible change. First they became quiet. Then they began averting their eyes. After a few minutes, they were sitting completely still. No one took notes. No one looked at me.

Ordinarily I would read in such reactions that I was completely missing the students, that they were bored or disengaged for some reason. This was different. I could feel their physical tension as they worked to stay motionless. All at once one of the coeds bolted from the room in wracking sobs. I caught up with her before she reached the end of the hall, and asked her to wait for me in my office where we could talk privately. I went back and picked up my lecture where I had left off. Again, no one moved. Another student bolted. I had him wait in the faculty lounge.

So it went. What they were doing was a common form of withdrawal. This is true not only of the ones who physically fled the room, but also those who stayed but refused to make eye contact. Unlike rage, which is a flatly *confrontive* emotion, withdrawal takes off, splits, gets out of there. And unlike rage, which has few nuances and no subtleties, withdrawal can clothe itself in a veritable showman's trunk of costumes and disguises. Sometimes it plays subtle by chilling out emotionally, as my students first did when they heard about the Shadow self. Sometimes withdrawal is the daggerman in a dark cape, lurking in the wings for its chance to take out the star on stage should the star somehow allow his mask to slip. When the strategy of withdrawal came for Karl, it came with a loaded gun.

Usually things aren't that dramatic, and withdrawal wears the costume of the traveler—not the tourist or the person with business to conduct, but the refugee, with disheveled hair, glazed over, weary eyes; and steamer trunks piled up all around. One can leave altogether, as happens when couples divorce, for example. The underlying dynamic in many divorces is withdrawal, but one has to ask what the person is withdrawing *from.* Sometimes the withdrawal is from a dangerous or degrading situation; or a situation of failed fidelity; or when the horseman, rage, has looted the marriage vows. But sometimes the dynamic is the reverse of what we present to the world. During courtship and dating we naturally put our best foot forward; we share our most attractive selves. The pressure cooker of marriage can steam off the glue that holds our masks in place, and we hear ourselves murmuring something like, "You're not the person I married." Of course, what has happened is that we have discovered the whole person we married, as we sometimes say, "warts and all." The commonest way people talk about their divorce is to identify the warts they discovered in the other person, and justify leaving by those warts. But I suspect that just as often the angry parties leave because in the behaviors of the spouse, and in their responses to those behaviors, they find their *own* warts—their Shadow selves—exposed. The shame issues involved can be so overwhelming that the offended party may even sabotage the marriage rather than risk further exposure. The breakup of the marriage is a hidden strategy to recover the mask and put it firmly back in place.

Withdrawal was also John's solution to the campaign of gossip that was waged against him by the organist at his church. He resigned, feeling dazed and puzzled about whether or not he was called into the ministry after all.

## The Horseman of Power

When John left the church, one of the reasons he gave was that he didn't want to do battle with the third horseman of the inner apocalypse—power. And power, as we have seen, was exactly what the organist was intending to use. Indeed, of Kaufman's four responses to shame, the most amenable to gossip as a weapon is the strategizing of power. But gossip is not the only way we wield power. Like withdrawal, power may come packaged in a wide variety of forms, ranging in depth and impact from emotional withdrawal to rumor mongering, to outright violence. When

David appeared at my door with Lori, he was clearly ready to punch my lights out—a brutal but unmistakable use of power to deal with their inner Shadows.

Another way of exercising power is to make sure one climbs to the top of whatever organizational heap one is in. Kaufman points out that the earliest experiences of shaming—and thus the emotional contours of the Shadow self—happen to us when we are children, sometimes so early that we are preverbal. Father is humiliated at work, but can't realistically do anything about it without jeopardizing his position, so he's edgy when he gets home. He takes his edginess out on Mother, who takes it out on the kid. And where does it end? With the youngest or smallest, that is, with whoever is the most vulnerable person in the system. And that youngest and smallest person is also the one with the narrowest range of resources for dealing with the shame.

It does not take many such experiences before a child can come to realize that there's a price to pay for being the smallest and most vulnerable. So on a deeply seated emotional level, perhaps even on a level that's difficult to verbalize, the child develops a need to climb to the top of the heap. When power is exercised in this way it does not solve the problem of the underlying feelings of shame or the dynamic movements of the Shadow; it merely serves as a kind of stopgap against exposure. The higher you go up the power hierarchy, the less vulnerable you are to shaming from above.

Perhaps the expression of power that is most difficult to see is the unwillingness or inability to forgive someone who has hurt us. In a careful appropriation of Kaufman's thoughts on shame, pastoral caregiver John Patton describes a conversation with a client named Tom who was expressing difficulty forgiving his father. The following exchange occurs after Tom tells Patton that he had gotten a lump in his throat after talking with his dad:

Pastor: "What's the lump? Discovering that he had problems too?"

Tom: "Wondering if I really can forgive him."

Pastor: "It's hard to give up that power."

Tom: "Power?"[2]

The power Patton had in view was the power that comes from the inability or the refusal to forgive. On a deep subconscious level, Tom knew that to forgive would make him vulnerable to his father again, and, conversely, by withholding forgiveness he would be able to retain the power to control the terms of any relationship there might be in the future. "In twenty years of pastoral counseling I have heard Tom's 'I don't know whether or not I can forgive' again and again and only recently have been able to call it what I think it is: a self-protective use of power."[3]

The refusal or inability to forgive also exerts control, not only over the relationship, but in some ways also directly over the person who has hurt us. In a famous study entitled *The Human Condition*, Hannah Arendt reflects on the importance of forgiveness for our ability to move forward with dignity:

> Without being forgiven, released from the consequences of what we have done, our capacity to act would, as it were, be confined to one single deed from which we could never recover; we would remain victims of its consequences.[4]

People need forgiveness to get on with their lives. Thus, when I withhold forgiveness from someone who has hurt me, I may be inflicting damage of my own. The unwillingness to forgive can have the exact same consequence as violence committed with malicious intent. And if the hurt is deep enough, I may turn from the horseman of power to gallop off the scene with the horseman of withdrawal. "Good-bye and good riddance!"

Thus, for Patton, forgiving involves giving up the power that comes with withholding forgiveness. It's particularly difficult to give up that power to someone who has hurt us—what if they hurt us again? That's why forgiveness cannot be coerced by an act of the will, but must be released, Patton says, as an act of grace.

The organist's power move of choice was injustice collecting, and she passed her collection on down the grapevine. It's interesting that throughout the entire episode, she never once spoke to John directly or even indicated that there were unresolved issues between them. Why, I wonder? I suspect that she was afraid that in such a conversation she would find herself exposed and vulnerable, perhaps even that John would be able to see things about her that she did not want seen. When she arranged for another minister to be on hand to preach in the event that John should resign, he took that as his cue to make his exit from the stage. He told me later that he didn't want to preside over a church split as the legacy of his first pastoral appointment.

## The Horseman of Perfectionism

The fourth horseman of the inner life is perfectionism. When I was a boy, my father kept an old garage, a free standing building in the rear of our property. It was a dirty place, the sort of garage where dust settled into the pools of oil in the floor, and tools were piled up randomly in old cardboard boxes along one wall. One hot summer day when I was perhaps nine or ten, I decided to clean my father's garage as a surprise. He was at work, and I was home for summer vacation. I thought it would be a nice gift. Apparently it wasn't nice enough, because when my father got home and saw that I hadn't cleaned the garage perfectly he found me and beat me for quitting too soon. I still remember what he said to me: "What counts isn't what you've done, but what there is left to do. After all," he said, "anything worth doing is worth doing well." Then he made me go back and work until he could run a white cloth across the floor and come up clean.

From that experience I learned two things: First, never volunteer, and second, if you don't want to be beaten, do it perfectly the first time. What happened to me in this extreme form is communicated to children all the time indirectly, by the things their parents say around them as they talk: "If those kids were mine, I'd beat the daylights out of them."

When Ann-Marie heard her father scapegoat her brother Kenneth, the effect was subtle, but the same. Remember that the reason she was in such distress was that she had received a "B" on a research paper. She knew rationally that a "B" is a good grade, something better than the norm. But what good are norms to someone who has to be perfect? What was good enough for somebody else was certainly not good enough for her. She was *better* than all of that. She *had* to be.

Indeed, in our quest for perfection, it little matters whether or not perfection as we envision it is even attainable. In a strikingly frank moment of self-disclosure, writer Sallie Tisdale comments on her own struggle to order her life around the ideal of physical beauty she saw in the pages of the popular women's magazines , even though she knew that those same images are regularly altered to eliminate flaws:

> Today's models, the women whose pictures I see constantly, unavoidably, grow more minimal every day. When I berate myself for not looking like—whomever I think I should look like that day, I don't really care that no one looks like that. . . . I want to look—think I should look—like the photographs. I want her (the model's) little miracles, the make-up artists, photographers, and computer imagers who can add a mole, remove a scar, lift the breasts, widen the eyes, narrow the hips, flatten the curves. The final product is what I see, have seen, my whole adult life.[5]

For Tisdale and others like her who suffer from eating disorders in the quest of physical perfection, the failure of that ideal—and it cannot help but fail—is the source of much torment of heart. But of course, physical beauty is only one weapon in this horseman's arsenal. The number of others is infinite because we can invent them as we need them. Ann-Marie's torment rested in the damage a "B" would bring to her perfect grade point average, Karl's on his inability to feel accepted and "normal" in a heterosexual world. For those who are caught up in the horseman of perfectionism, failure can produce long, internal spasms of anguish, spasms that might as well be apocalyptic for all the savage impact they can have on the self.

### When the Horsemen Raid Together

These, then, are the four horsemen of the inner apocalypse: rage, withdrawal, power, and perfectionism. But they do not always ride into our spiritual lives alone. They sometimes appear together. I can envision them arranging themselves like a wedge configuration a football team might make to protect the quarterback. If you run the wedge in tight formation, shoulder to shoulder, you create a little pocket in which the quarterback has room to maneuver without danger of being tackled. A good coach knows to put the strongest player on the point of the wedge. In the battle to protect the Shadow, some of us prefer to put rage on the point, backed up on one side with withdrawal, and on the other side with power or perfectionism. But there are a wide number of fluid configurations we can run.

While we have our preferred point of defense, we can shift strategies if need be and array our troops in different configurations. The strategy adopted by Kenneth, Ann-Marie's scapegoated brother, was to place withdrawal on the point, backed up by power and rage. Each time he found himself triangled out of the family unit, he had to make a decision about how he would respond. Whatever other options were open to him, he found that by withdrawing from the family but refusing to comply with his parents' expectations, he was able to exert enormous control over the movement of power in the family. It was disruptive control to be sure, but it preserved his sense of internal equilibrium by masking his sense of shame at the way he was being treated.

It's important that the four horsemen of the inner apocalypse are in the business of covering up something else. They can create enormous problems in human relationships, but that doesn't change their role in defending against shame. Indeed, it's the shame that gives them their ability to hold our inner lives hostage, stuck in the spiderwebs of inner crisis. You can hardly say, "quit being such a perfectionist," or "so forgive already." That's because the perfectionism or the inability to forgive play important roles in maintaining our sense of inner equilibrium. To give them up can be threatening because it can cost us our sense of who we are.

It's also important to remember that these are common human responses to a common human problem. The Shadow self isn't particularly a *religious* problem at all. It's clear enough, and common enough, to see these as psychological maladies, character disorders for which what is needed is therapy or involvement in a twelve-step program. Or, perhaps in their milder forms, just as troublesome moods and dispositions to be dealt with as they appear.

The need to be right. The need to dominate. The need to be perfect. The terror of having to face the uncomfortable self-disclosure that true community requires. When the four horsemen of the inner apocalypse ride into our lives they can make demands that edge out completely the realities of grace. When that happens, they have become, not additional sources of guidance and direction, but *competing* ones, functioning like religions in their own right.

What happens to these normal human tendencies when we add in theological language—the promise of heaven and the threat of hell, biblical authority, and the righteous indignation of the saints? When the chips are down and our backs are to the wall, most of us turn out to be street fighters; we use every weapon we can to gain the upper hand in the fight. A bully picks a fight, and we grab a two-by-four; the other guy has a gun, we break a bottle. For those of us whose life experience includes religious commitments and values, the language of faith can be a really useful weapon in the street fight of life. Rage is one thing, but rage that's justified by biblical language can be all the more effective. How much more powerful it is to refuse to forgive when we believe we have the Bible, or God, or principles of justice on our side! Perfectionism is one thing, but perfectionism that's backed up by *righteousness* is another thing altogether. Weapons honed on the whetstone of righteous indignation can be wicked sharp!

When we use the vocabulary of faith and the authority of Scripture as tools to validate our rage, buttress our power, affirm our perfection, or justify our withdrawal, the result has an intensifying effect on all of the issues involved. What happens when we use such language to build up the root metaphors for spirituality that govern the life of our churches? We teach each other and, more importantly, our children a certain way of thinking about and experiencing our faith. We come to believe that this is right, perhaps even biblical, because it can come to feel normal. At the same time, we may be building a common life in which there are dangers on every hand, a common life in which desperate people—people like Karl—have no other way to deal with their inner agonies than to resolve them with a gun.

CHAPTER ELEVEN

# CHRISTOS ALETHOS ANISTI

## The Four Winds of the Spiritual Life

*The wind blows where it chooses, and you hear the sound of it, but you do not know where it comes from or where it goes. So it is with everyone who is born of the Spirit.*
—John 3:8

When I was a young man, before I started college, I left home and for a year and a half traveled with a touring musical production called *Up with People!* I also left my parents' faith behind, not because I was rebellious, but because I was disappointed. The standards were just too low. My perfectionism demanded something sturdier. At that time, *Up with People!* was sponsored by an organization called Moral Re-Armament, an idealist movement that promoted social change through courageous self-examination. The "compass points" of that self-examination were four moral standards, which we considered absolutely binding on human experience—honesty, unselfishness, purity, and love.

Each night before going on stage, we would bolster one another in the greenroom with talk about our dreams of a better world; we would hold our own ideals up for examination by the group. One night I took the floor. I spoke briefly but eloquently—or so I thought—about the four moral standards, about the needs of our fallen, drifting world, about the wisdom we had to teach, and about educating the audience about values. The moral standards were absolutely binding, you could hold them in your hand, they were *granite*.

When I finished, the leader of the group, a young man named Ken, dropped me in my tracks. "Hoggatt," he said, "you say a heck of a lot, but you don't do a darned thing."

He nailed me. He had me dead to rights. But he shocked me because all my life, in one form or another, I have tried very hard to "do a darn thing." As I write this chapter about the responses Christian spirituality makes to the problems of the Shadow self, I bring with me to my task the stinging memory of Ken's direct and honest rebuke, and I imagine him now reading this manuscript and thinking perhaps the same thing.

In chapter 10 we caught a short glimpse of what I have called "the four horsemen of the inner apocalypse"—withdrawal, perfectionism, rage, and the abuse of power. These four great psychological warriors can sweep across the spiritual landscape the way Grant swept through the American South with his scorched earth policy of destroying everything in his path.

In this battle, the horsemen are not fighting for themselves. These warriors are not crusaders, so much as conscripts, mercenaries hired to fight a battle not their own, but still absolutely merciless in return for their pay. Their master and overlord is none other than the Shadow self.

Each of the horsemen is a mask we wear to cover our Shadow and keep it hidden from public view. At the end of the last chapter I said that when we add theological ideas and language into the mix, the stakes are raised all around. The color can be forced out of life and the gray that remains becomes black and white. Rage becomes righteous indignation. The quest for perfection—impossible in its own right—

can come to be holier-than-thou piety. If we pose this as a spiritual problem, we could say that the four horsemen of the inner apocalypse are the way we lie to ourselves about our own need of grace.

It would be right, then, to ask what the Christian traditions of spirituality have to say in response.. An answer to that question comes from the writings of a Marian monk named Ronald Rolheiser. In a book entitled, *The Holy Longing*, Rolheiser explores the nature and history of spirituality in the Western Christian traditions, both Catholic and Protestant. This is not a simple task. The world, says Rolheiser, is filled with "spiritualities." Just think of how many movements and institutions call themselves by the name *Christian*. We could list them, though no matter how many pages we took the list would be instantly incomplete because new spiritualities are being born by the minute. Such a list would need to include everything from the Desert Fathers to the Promise Keepers—monastic groups, soldiers marching under Christian flags during the Crusades, charismatic groups, the Anabaptist movement, the Salvation Army, Pentecostals, evangelical groups, the Moral Majority, the Christian Coalition, the Episcopal Church, the Catholic Gay Rights Movement, feminist theology, Wycliffe Bible Translators, The New Tribes Mission, liberation theology, postmodern theology, social justice groups, and fundamentalism.

Each of these groups has its own distinctive brand of spirituality; each has its own "hermeneutic," its own way of moving from event to story. Each is its own spiritual climate zone and could probably readily say what's wrong with everyone else's spirituality. Yet all claim to be Christian. Surely there must be some common denominator. But what?

Rolheiser rephrases this question by drawing a theological distinction between *essential* truth and *accidental* truth. An essential truth is "necessary for everyone, prescribed for everyone, and nonnegotiable for everyone."[1] Essential truths are truths that can be ignored or contradicted only at our peril. Accidental truth is "real truth, but . . . truth that takes its importance only in relationship to more essential truth."[2] The truth of Jesus' resurrection has a different sort of significance than the truth of, say, the location of his grave. With this distinction in hand, Rolheiser asks, in the quest for substance and balance, what are the truths that are somehow *essential* to Christian spirituality? What are those aspects of the spiritual life that are necessary, prescribed, and nonnegotiable for everyone? What are those that we neglect to our peril?

Rolheiser proposes four nonnegotiable elements of the spiritual life—personal piety and personal morality, the practice of social justice, mellowness of spirit, and life in community. Each of these, he says, is a *pillar* of Christian spirituality.

I prefer a slightly different image, that of wind. Winds seem somehow harder to possess and more elusive. Wind can be actively resisted, where pillars cannot. Pillars are *things*, wind is *movement*. There is no wind without change. "The wind blows where it chooses," Jesus said, "and you hear the sound of it, but you do not know where it comes from or where it goes. So it is with everyone who is born of the Spirit" (John 3:8).

So the image I bring is wind, not pillars. Wind cannot be captured, it isn't something we can own; it must be taken on its own terms. It's elusive, invisible, and impossible to pin down. So, too, is the life of the Spirit.

## The Spiritual Wind of Commitment to Community

For the inner apocalypse horseman of withdrawal, the essential wind of the spirit is commitment to community.

It's not difficult to see how withdrawal damages community. When we leave a community because of our wounds we take our hurt with us but we often leave the community itself wounded in our wake. The ugliest form of this is when whole churches split, but the damage is the same when individuals leave—emotionally or physically.

But the reverse of this image is also true. Just as withdrawal works against community, so community can serve as an active redemptive force against withdrawal. In community we can, as the Bible says, "bear one another's burdens."

Burdens there are, and the manner in which we bear them tells us something important about the kinds of forces that hold our community together. According to psychiatrist Scott Peck, we only form community by sticking out the tough times. Indeed, it is the tough times that make community possible. Once, when my wife was away at a meeting, my four-year-old daughter and I decided to surprise her with an apple pie. I learned an important lesson that night: You can't double the temperature and cut the cooking time in half. Some things can only be made by slow cooking. In our world of instant gratification we tend to think of community on the analogy of a salad, nourishing and light, but tossed together, with some kind of oil to bind the flavors. Genuine community is more of a roast; it has substance to it, it's more nourishing, has better flavor and richer aroma, but it has to be pounded and seared and slow-cooked into existence. You can't double the temperature and halve the time.

This is true of a good many social relationships. There are all kinds of groups that form true community on this model—Kiwanis Clubs, Boy Scout troops, rock climbing expeditions, or the women's movement. So what is it that makes the community of the church genuinely Christian, rather than just another social group with a long history of shared troubles and triumphs?

Jesus provides an answer: "By this everyone will know that you are my disciples, if you have love for one another" (John 13:35). Paul answers it, too, with his image of the church as the body of Christ. True Christian community is, in part, deference to one another out of reverence for Christ.

But there is more, I think. During my travels with *Up*

*with People!* the members of our cast had been billeted with various families and it happens that I was placed in the home of the cook at a Byzantine Catholic monastery in Stamford, Connecticut. It was Easter, and my host family invited me to join them in the monastery chapel for midnight mass. The room was tiny and was crowded with perhaps thirty or forty worshipers. I was nearly overwhelmed by the smell of the burning incense. The flickering golden light of the candles was the only light in the room. The monks filed in and began the mass. They chanted a cappella for more than an hour in some foreign language—Russian I think. I didn't understand a word of it.

At one point the monks filtered out into the congregation to exchange the traditional Easter greeting: *Christos anisti*—Christ has risen. Back came the reply: *Alethos anisti*—He has truly risen!

One monk suddenly made a beeline to the back door where there was a huge bull of a man standing a little hesitant, just come in from the blustery wind. He had a thick red-gold beard and long hair, blown all awry. As I recall it now, it seems he had leaves in his hair. He looked like the mad Russian monk Rasputin, except his eyes were calm. He paused by the door as though he was unsure of where he was or if he should come in. My host whispered to me that he had left the monastery and this was his first time to return.

The monk approached the giant: *Christos anisti.* The giant couldn't reply; he just stood there speechless. He hesitated a moment, then threw his massive arms around the monk, buried his face in his shoulder, and sobbed, *Christos alethos anisti—Christ has truly risen!*

That was the precise moment I decided that I could be a Christian. If Christ has not risen, then nothing matters. If *Christos alethos anisti*, then nothing else matters in quite the same way. It is the resurrection that makes it possible for the church to be the body of Christ in reality, rather than merely in metaphor. The granite hard fact of the resurrection breathes its life into the church and makes it somehow more and different than a gathering of people who have endured hard times together.

Christian community is sometimes based on something other—on personal loyalty to a gifted preacher, on fear of being scapegoated, on the false sense of security that comes from triangling our friends, on doctrinal commitments, on shared taboos, on shared tribal language, on a history of shared troubles, or on the fact that we come from the same social and economic groups. To the extent that this is so, the community may very well be true community, but it is not the church.

How, I wonder, does the reality of the resurrection affect the talk within the churches? What does this mean for the conversation over the back fence? How do we make that reality a matter for deliberate practice, rather than a matter of mere habit?

For starters we can keep confidences. We can remember that because every story must leave something out, every tidbit of gossip could be artfully and truly told in a different version. More than anything, we can recognize that the power of speech is a genuine power, something that can be used for evil, but also turned to good. When our talk creates artificial boundaries that keep people out of the church, it is not morally neutral, but is a pact with the devil. It is something for which we need forgiveness and healing. But when our talk batters down the walls that keep people out, then it is a way of participating in the reality of redemption.

## The Spiritual Wind of Justice

For the Abuse of Power horseman, the wind of Christian spirituality is the search for justice.

Within the Christian tradition, the quest for justice has always had two prongs—concern for the individuals who have been damaged by the abuses of power, and concern about the social structures that made it possible for there to be abuse in the first place. Although these two prongs are closely interconnected, in actuality they are practiced with different levels of attention and skill in the various sectors of the church. Christians on the left seem to attend to the matter of social justice on a global scale, dealing like modern-day prophets with government agencies and legislation, while Christians on the right tend instead to deal with individuals and the personal circumstances in which they sometimes find themselves.

The search for justice has its own validity, of course. It's something we should seek for its own sake. Everyone, Christian or not, ought to seek justice because it makes for a fairer and more equitable world. But Christians have another reason.

Within the Old Testament, concern for justice finds its most urgent and compelling voices in the writings of the prophets. It is an unmistakable message: An infallible indicator of the spiritual health of a society is the manner in which its most vulnerable members are faring. In the case of the Bible, this group includes the orphan, the widow, and the sojourner in the land.

The New Testament takes this principle a step further. Not only are Christians asked to aid the vulnerable, we are asked to become vulnerable with them. The gospel account where this new principle of servant leadership is most clearly set out is in Mark 10:42-45.

> So Jesus called them and said to them, "You know that among the Gentiles those whom they recognize as their rulers lord it over them, and their great ones are tyrants over them. But it is not so among you; but whoever wishes to become great among you must be your servant, and whoever wishes to be first among you must be slave of all."

What is important about this passage is the reason for servant leadership given at the end of the section in verse 45:

"For the Son of Man came not to be served but to serve, and to give his life a ransom for many."

In his own way, Paul too understood this principle. In a famous passage in Philippians 2:5-8 Paul reflects on the meaning of the incarnation:

> Let the same mind be in you that was in Christ Jesus, who, though he was in the form of God, did not regard equality with God as something to be exploited, but emptied himself, taking the form of a slave, being born in human likeness. And being found in human form, he humbled himself and became obedient to the point of death—even death on a cross.

This passage is famous for what it says about the deity of Christ. After all, this is a good demonstration of something theologians call a high Christology. But that's not what the passage is about. Both before and after, Paul tells the Philippians to serve one another as Christ did. Paul's point is that if Jesus, who had the form of God, can take the form of a servant, *how much more* ought Christians do the same. It's in this same spirit that the letter to the Ephesians tells Christian husbands to "love your wives, just as Christ loved the church and gave himself up for her" (5:25). If Christ has sacrificed so much for us, how much more ought we to sacrifice for one another!

The point here is twofold. First, within the tradition of biblical faith, justice is nonnegotiable. Second, the practice of justice is the Christian tradition's answer to the abuse of power. According to the Bible, the practice of justice is an absolutely reliable indicator of the state of our soul, and in the final judgment will be a criterion of our faithfulness to God. Not only must the Christian seek justice for its own sake, but also simply because God is a God of justice.

How, I wonder, does the quest for justice affect the Christian's talk over the back fence? On a wall above my desk are painted the words, *auditur et altera pars:* Let the other side also be heard. We can seek the whole truth. We can break triangles, and at the same time recognize that those who triangle are in need of care. We can find those who have been scapegoated out and, like the shepherd who finds a lost sheep, we can gather them up and bring them back in, home to the safety of the fold.

Let me urge one final caution: The practice of justice sometimes leads to bitterness of heart. We may make a decision with the best of intentions, only to discover later that we did not know our own heart well enough, or conditions have changed, or the person for whom we have made some sacrifice has taken advantage of us. When that happens, it's hard not to feel cheated, and we can end up angry with God and bitter at ourselves. There must be something in the mix that can take the edge off. With that in mind, we turn to the third wind of the spiritual life—mellowness of heart and spirit.

### The Spiritual Wind of Joy

For the perfectionist horseman the wind of the spiritual life is something Rolheiser calls mellowness of heart and spirit. This is surprising language from a monk, indeed, it would be surprising from anyone who takes his or her religion seriously. In the tradition in which I was reared, religion is marked out by *gravity*, by the seriousness of the fallen situation in which we find ourselves. As a youth I was attracted by Christians who could celebrate life without apology—attracted, but frightened, too.

But for Rolheiser, mellowness of heart and spirit is a non-negotiable of the spiritual life. The world we know is so full of hurts, wounds, violence, and sins, so much a place of injustice, that celebration seems to be fundamentally out of place, much less a *norm*. And yet, Rolheiser insists. As badly as the world needs justice, it also needs joy.

He illustrates with the example of Jesus, or rather, with a story in which the example of Jesus proves to be the key. It appears that there was a young nun of his acquaintance, whose spiritual life was exemplary in every way. She regularly practiced the disciplines of prayer and confession, went to mass every day, and was an active, serious member of her community, which had dedicated itself to the service of the poor.

Rolheiser met this nun at a conference on the ministry of the church. The work in the conference had been grueling and after several days the moderator had called a break. They would take an afternoon off, see the sights of the city, stroll along the river, and meet in the evening for a meal at the Holiday Inn. So it happened—for everyone except the nun. She stayed in the bus and sulked. Later, she commented:

> I walked into the restaurant, saw all the silver knives and forks and the linen serviettes, and I became nauseated and couldn't go through with it. So I went out and sat on the bus and waited while everyone else ate.
>
> But I had to sit there a long time. Many thoughts ran through my head, and at one stage I asked myself the question: "Would Jesus be in there eating and drinking and having a good time?" And I had the horrible realization that he would be! John the Baptist—with his leather belt and his grasshoppers!—would be with me on the bus, boycotting all this joy in the name of the poor. I realized that . . . I had become the older brother of the prodigal son, doing all the right things, but having no celebration in my heart.[3]

Here, then, is the Christian tradition's response to the horseman of perfectionism. C. S. Lewis once remarked that a ship can fail on its journey in either of two ways—it can sink en route, or it can arrive at the wrong port. Perfectionists may well succeed in keeping their lives in line and still fail miserably at following the lead of Jesus, the Lord of the dance, the life of the party.

I caught a tiny glimpse of this reality in the Byzantine Catholic monastery. The mass had ended, and the members of the congregation filtered out of the chapel and into the refectory where there was a celebration breakfast waiting. How we feasted that Easter morning! There were decorated eggs and special pastries. There were rolls by the basketful, and a thirty-pound Easter egg made of butter, with Byzantine religious symbols pressed into the sides. There was fresh coffee and hand-squeezed orange juice. We talked and laughed and ate kielbasa until we were stuffed. What a wonderful way to follow the celebration of Easter, or so I thought, but my host corrected me. "Perhaps not in letter, but certainly in spirit, the party doesn't come *after* the mass," he said. "It's *part* of it."

How does mellowness of heart and spirit affect the Christian's life of gossip? It adds zest, it encourages, and it brings the healing balm of laughter. It says, to all of us who struggle with the heavy burden of perfectionism, *lighten up. Christos alethos anisti.*

But not everyone knows how to lighten up. Karl Olsson sounds a cautionary note: Sometimes Christians who know how to celebrate frighten those who don't:

> The Bible is a party full of merriment and red balloons. . . . It abounds in party clothes, perfumes, and ointments; in music, dancing, and frolic. Jesus came and wherever he went there was a party, "the feast of the bridegroom" (Luke 7:31-34).
>
> But the Bible is also filled with jealous eyes and malicious hearts. . . . There are fasters who think ill of feasters. There are workers who think ill of partyers. There are brothers who never made it, hating the brother who did.[4]

### The Spiritual Wind of Personal Piety and Personal Morality

We are brought then to the horseman of rage whose answering wind of the spirit is personal piety and personal morality. By personal piety, Rolheiser means something close to what an evangelical might mean by the phrase "personal relationship with Jesus Christ," but he means that somewhat more broadly. Personal piety and personal morality include our habits of prayer and Bible study, the disciplines by which we deepen our spirituality, and the attention we pay to the demands of the moral life on a personal, individual, human scale.

What have such things to do with rage? On the surface of it, this is a long stretch. How do we move from one to the other? As we saw in chapter 10, rage is a common response to our feelings of exposure. It can be a way of backing down the person who has exposed us, and in that way protecting the Shadow from further discovery. To set down the rage I must first be willing to face the hurt or the shame that the rage is masking.

Pastoral caregiver John Patton explores this same problem in terms of the terrible difficulty we face if we are ever going to forgive those who have hurt us. We cannot forgive, says Patton, without encountering once again the hurt that has been inflicted upon us, without feeling the knife in our heart, the blow to our pride, the raw and sometimes bleeding wound from which our refusal to forgive has somehow protected us. When we forgive we stagger under the blow all over again. That is why forgiveness is not an act of the will, but a discovery of grace. Forgiveness isn't something we can order into existence.

Rage and grace are opposite drives, like the positive and negative poles of a magnet. One repels, the other attracts, but they never live quietly in the same person. That is why Jesus instructs his followers, "whenever you stand praying, forgive, if you have anything against anyone; so that your Father in heaven may also forgive you your trespasses" (Mark 11:25). If we don't genuinely forgive, but simply pretend that all is well, we can turn the anger inward and do damage to our own inner lives.

How does personal piety work its way in our daily talk?

In some small way, it looks for the redemptive perspective that can restore the broken heart and bring healing where there are hurts. A classic example of such piety is found in Victor Hugo's novel, *Les Miserables*. Set during the turbulent years of the French Revolution, this is the story of an escaped convict named Jean Valjean, who was imprisoned and badly treated for stealing bread. One night after escaping prison, he is sheltered and fed by a Catholic bishop named M. Charles Francois-Bienvenu Myriel. In payment for this act of kindness, Valjean steals the man's silver service and slips away into the night. The world is so unfair, and the bishop will not suffer from the loss. Who will know? Except that the police soon catch Valjean and return him to the bishop's house for an explanation. The bishop holds Valjean's future in his hands. He does something absolutely unexpected—he tells the police that the silver service had been given to Valjean as a gift, and then he adds a pair of silver candlesticks for good measure.

After the police have left, the bishop makes this comment: "Jean Valjean, my brother: you belong no more to evil, but to good. It is your soul that I am buying for you. I withdraw it from dark thoughts and from the spirit of perdition, and I give it to God!"[5]

Thus he breaks the cycle of guilt and poverty, and by a single act of redemption places Jean Valjean's feet on a different and more honorable path. Bishop Myriel's action was born of a careful and sensitive understanding of the workings of the human soul. What is important here is that the bishop shows that he knows not only what to do and say, but also what *not* to do and say. As Edward Hays once remarked, some things it is better not to know, even if we must forget them forcefully.

### But Why Is It So Hard?

It seems like such a simple exchange. Trade alienation for reconciliation, trade power for justice, trade uptight perfectionism for a mellow and joyful spirit, trade rage for forgiveness. So much to gain, so little to lose. It should be so easy, a cakewalk.

But it's not. The reality is that it's hard. We resist with everything inside of us. As psychiatrist Nathaniel Brandon says, "But not every client *wants* to be rid of his pain. There are persons who cling to their pain as a precious possession, refusing to relinquish it, nurturing it like some sacred fire."[6] Sometimes the resistance takes the form of a deep yearning, a hunger for something more, but the sure sense that there isn't any way to get there.

This is especially so of the wind of mellowness of heart. As fifty-year-old Denise said to me only this week: "All my life I've known that the world is divided into two groups of people—the good people who go to church, and the bad people, who do not. So I have always gone to church, but in my heart I know that if the good people there ever find out what I'm really like inside they won't have anything to do with me." Denise came to me asking for a miracle—literally, those were her words—that would enable her to set down the heavy burden of her exile and find her way home. And yet the heavy burden was all that she had known.

Why the terrible resistance? I believe it comes in part because the four horsemen are in the service of a hidden agenda, the need to protect our Shadow selves from discovery at all costs. Shadows brought into light tend to disappear, and the resistances we feel are our inner selves pushing for their own preservation.

## The Underlying Reality of Grace

What Patton says of forgiveness applies with equal force to the four winds of the spirit. Just as we cannot simply order up forgiveness as an act of the will, so we cannot seek justice or community solely as an act of the will. We must invite the presence of God, must pay close attention to matters of justice, must nurture our gift for joy, and must open our windows and doors to the healing and redemptive winds of the

Spirit. When these things become real, when they take shape in our daily lives, they only do so as events of grace. Here then is the ultimate mystery of the practice of the Christian religion. It is something that we do, but something we cannot do, something we invite, but do not create, and when that happens, we have encountered grace.

I remember when the first time I began to move beyond my childhood understandings of grace. Throughout this book I have alluded to the difficulties I had from time to time with my father. My parents were divorced when I was twelve. Before my father left for his hometown, he took me for a fatherly talk; we sat on a log beside a dry creek bed. In this talk, my father told me that he blamed me for the ruin of his marriage, and that he was sorry I had ever been born.

My immediate response to this act of scapegoating was a silent vow: "I'll show this son of a b——." What I meant was that I would find some way to force my father to be proud of me. In time, that immediate response converted itself into a kind of secret mission statement, complete with theological overtones. I would force *God* to be proud of me, and to do so I would become a "super-Christian," I would somehow combine evangelistic power with intellectual precision. I would do it all. Like Ann-Marie in chapter 9, I would go for the golden ring.

There is no better fertilizer for a rigid and uptight perfectionism. The problem was, not only was I miserable in my faith, I had missed faith altogether. Neurotic perfectionism is based on the faulty idea that we can do for God what God insists on doing for us. It is a way of thumbing our nose at grace. I remember breaking out in chills while reading this passage from a little book with the intriguing title, *Come to the Party*. The author, Karl Olsson, was describing a moment I so desperately needed.

> Some time in the summer of 1967, [I came] face-to-face with the real me and suddenly discovered that we are justified by

> faith alone and not works, "lest any man should boast." What this meant for *me*, quite practically, was that God had already accepted the real *me* in Christ and that I didn't have to be eaten up by malarial mosquitoes, slog through mud, contract dysentery, translate the Bible, swallow the mutterings and the up-tight rantings of paranoids, study the next move on the great religio-political chessboard, win every argument and every tennis game, speak to 50,000 people, read the Bible through eighteen times, pray for twenty-four hours at a stretch, balance the budget, be listed in *Who's Who*, empty bedpans, bridge the generation gap, be bored, be insulted, be tense, be tired—I did not, praise God in the highest, need to *do* any of these or *be* any of these in order to make it with God. I was free to be me and to be human.[7]

This is, I believe in the best possible sense, the answer I would now make to Ken, the leader of my cast of *Up with People!* Because *Christos alethos anisti*, I do not, praise God in the highest, need to *do* any of these or *be* any of these in order to make it with God. I am free to be me and to be human. In God's name I can set down the heavy granite burden of needing to do a darn thing.

CHAPTER TWELVE

# LIGHTNING BOLTS AND AQUIFERS

## What Goes Around Comes Around

*Look at ships: though they are so large that it takes strong winds to drive them, yet they are guided by a very small rudder wherever the will of the pilot directs. So also the tongue is a small member, yet it boasts of great exploits.*
—James 3:4-5

When I was in the third grade I was introduced for the first time to something Mrs. Gunn called the water cycle. We studied the water cycle in all kinds of ways. We made mason jar tornadoes and we tracked storms from reports in the newspapers. My favorite project was the pictures we drew—gray cumulous clouds, with slanting blue lines to represent rain, then rivers running through brown crayon mountain ranges, and then oceans with visible fish beneath the surface (mine had a mermaid, but it didn't help my grade), and waves represented by little flattened quarter moons of blue with sailboats resting gingerly on top.

The discovery of the water cycle carried with it a host of other discoveries, not least of which was that this part of the world was an interconnected whole, with loops and loops out there that I couldn't see. Mrs. Gunn said that we couldn't hope to understand the weather *today* unless we saw that it was connected to weather that had happened months earlier in a different part of the world. Then she said that the same thing was true about the rest of the environment—the logging of rain forests in Paraguay will someday have an effect on the quality of the rain in Indonesia, diesel fuel burned in Ohio will affect the drinking water in New Orleans.

Mrs. Gunn's explanation of the water cycle was accurate and appropriate for the third grade, but I've since learned that there are an extraordinary number of factors that she never mentioned, and that I may never see—the special properties of water, the temperature of the air at various elevations, the barometric pressure, and the location and depth of the aquifers.

In a sense, what we have been describing in this book is a cycle of influences that shape the social climate in which we work out our spirituality. That cycle looks something like this:

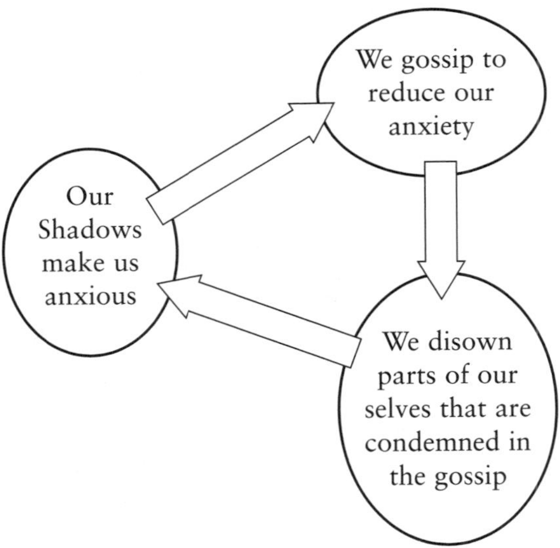

Like Mrs. Gunn's third-grade explanation of the water cycle, this one's simplified, and it leaves out a lot of other factors that run beneath the surface. Some of those factors I've mentioned elsewhere in this book—the specific properties of language, the social dynamics, the play of vested interests and unacknowledged anxieties, the reasons we gossip, the choices we make about who's safe to talk to and who's not, the rules of taboo about what we can say and how we can say it.

If we recognize the simplification and allow this little diagram to represent the whole, it provides us with a useful way of thinking about the spiritual atmosphere in which we live out our journeys of faith. Mrs. Gunn's explanation of the water cycle never mentioned the significance of the specific properties of *air*, but they were factors, too, just as the properties of the language we use are factors in the overall weather system of the church. And that's what we have here, really—a whole system of beliefs, motivations, hidden agendas, hopes and disappointments. The weather system of the church includes not only our most noble convictions, but also our deepest fears, our emotions, and the official and unofficial movement of power.

It also includes the disciplines of our spirituality, our yearning for a deeper personal relationship with God, our sometimes faltering attempts to bring about justice, our efforts at loyalty and devotion to the community of faith, and the delight in life—Reinholder's "mellowness of heart"—that seems to be a mark of genuine spirituality.

## The Cycles of Life Interconnect

The cycles interconnect. The number of student research papers I may have to grade in a given week impacts the frequency of my trips to the grocery store. The quality of breakfast a child had in the morning may significantly impact her ability to master a complex math problem at school. The harsh, judgmental tone in a parent's voice may ring for years in the head of her child, impacting the child's sense of self-worth and value.

The largest cycles may take generations or even centuries before they play themselves out. In the life of the church, there are cycles of spiritual deadness and cycles of renewal, cycles in which we have lost our bearings because of the constant pull of the issues of the world, or our own inner need to be right, to dominate, or to be perfect. Some of those cycles are the result of the difficult choices we have to make as we live out our faith in the world of work, in government, in the schools, and in our homes. Some of them are the result of interactions with our own inner lives: what happens to us, our *take* on what happens to us, the choices we ourselves make by way of response, the things we say to ourselves to validate our position, the things we say to everyone else to validate our position, and then what happens to us as a consequence. All this forms great swirling eddies of influences. And in it all, the four horsemen of the inner apocalypse—rage, withdrawal, power, and perfectionism—are not only the volcanoes, earthquakes, and firestorms of our spiritual climate, they're also false poles that give false readings to our internal moral and spiritual compasses.

One important example of this interconnected system is the context in which we come to terms with the meaning of Scripture. If the gossip of the church is filled with talk about why slavery is morally right, then the argument that the Bible favors slavery will somehow *feel* more satisfying, and will be more likely to be taken as compelling. If the talk emphasizes equality between husbands and wives, the interpretations of Scripture that favor subordination will feel odd and out of whack. We are more easily persuaded that something is biblical if it's in line with what we came to believe from the weather system of the gossip.

Usually all of this takes place on a small scale because much of the world of talk operates like tiny cycles of the weather. In chapter 4, we saw that when children talk together on the playground, they make subtle adjustments in the ways they tell their stories so their peers will believe the stories. They tell with one finger raised to the prevailing social winds. Talk—watch for reactions—adjust story—talk. A tiny cycle of testing, observation, change, testing.

But we do this in larger cycles, too. Thirty years ago one of the religion faculty at our university was dismissed for having an inappropriate liaison with a student. Recently his name came up in a lunchroom conversation, and when new faculty asked who he was, the answer came back automatically: He used to teach religion here, but was dismissed for sexual misconduct. Memory can have a long reach, and—at least on our campus—the consequences of that single poor decision will be with him for the rest of his life.

### Leverage

But it does not have to be that way. Sometimes the stories can be redemptive, can salvage us from the damage we have done to ourselves. Some time after third grade I learned a second important principle about cycles, the principle of *leverage*. If a cycle is made up of interconnected parts, sometimes a change in a minor part can yield a change in the cycle as a whole, and thus a change in a major part. Leverage is the ability to bring about major changes in outcomes by making minor, carefully focused changes elsewhere in the cycle, like seeding a storm or damming a river. MIT systems analyst Peter Senge explains leverage in terms of the rudder on a ship:

> If you knew absolutely nothing about hydrodynamics and you saw a large oil tanker plowing through the high seas, where would you push if you wanted the tanker to turn left? You would probably go to the bow and try and push to the left. Do you have any idea how much force it takes to turn an oil tanker going fifteen knots by pushing on its bow? The

> leverage lies in going to the stern and pushing the tail end of the tanker to the right, in order to turn the front to the left. This, of course, is the job of the rudder. But in what direction does the rudder turn in order to get the ship's stern to turn to the right? Why, to the left, of course.
>
> You see, ships turn because their rear end is "sucked around." The rudder, by being turned into the oncoming water, compresses the water flow and creates a pressure differential. The pressure differential pulls the stern in the opposite direction as the rudder is turned. [1]

But in modern ships, even the rudder can be too massive to move easily, so nautical engineers have added a refinement, a rudder for the rudder, called a *trim tab*.

> The trim tab—this very small device that has an enormous effect on a huge ship—does the same for the rudder. When it is turned to one side or another, it compresses the water flowing around the rudder and creates a small pressure differential that "sucks the rudder" in the desired direction. But, if you want the rudder to turn to the left, what direction do you turn the trim tab?—to the right, naturally.[2]

This thick description emphasizes Senge's conclusion that before one can decide on the best point of leverage, one first has to understand the workings of the system as a whole, and that may call for careful observation and thought. Often more is going on than meets the eye. In the human experience, that something more is often hidden beneath the masks we wear to keep even redemptive eyes from prying.

Often, says Senge, effects are only distantly related to their causes, through loop after loop of interacting cycles and sub-cycles, so "areas of highest leverage are often least obvious."[3] Surely this is so in the difficult area of human relationships and talk, in which so much of what is really going on is hidden by our masks. Senge continues:

> Business and other human endeavors are also systems. They, too, are bound by invisible fabrics of interrelated actions, which often take years to fully play out their effects on each other. Since we are part of that lacework ourselves, it's doubly hard to see the whole pattern of change. Instead, we tend to focus on snapshots of isolated parts of the system, and wonder why our deepest problems never seem to get solved.[4]

Because of leverage, different events have different levels of bearing on a problem, and sometimes a single event can leverage everything into a fresh framework. In chapter 11 we discussed a scene from Victor Hugo's novel, *Les Miserables* in which bishop Charles Francois-Bienvenu Myriel "rescues" the criminal Jean Valjean by telling the authorities that the silver table service Valjean has stolen was really a gift. Here is a classic illustration of leverage in human relationships. In the larger scheme of things, the bishop's gift and the words he used to explain it are like a trim-tab on the rudder of Jean Valjean's otherwise rudderless ship; they set his life on an entirely different course. The good bishop leveraged Valjean's fate to good.

Most of the time, leverage is less dramatic. It works its way because of the interconnections it makes with other leveraging events. I still remember an offhanded comment made by one of the motivational speakers they brought to speak to my seventh-grade class. The speaker was talking about breaking the cycles of anger and recrimination that sometimes plague families. He said he had been driving on the freeway when someone in the next lane cut him off in a bid for an off-ramp. It was a reckless maneuver, and he had cursed the man under his breath.

His wife's response leveraged him into a completely different perspective: "I happen to know for a fact," she said, "that he's rushing to the hospital. His wife's giving birth in the backseat."

"She didn't know that," the speaker told us, "but it might have been true. The truth was, I didn't know what had motivated that man to cut me off. I didn't know enough to be that angry. So I let it go. I've been letting things go ever since."

It was an offhanded remark, not part of his planned presentation, and it was made nearly forty years ago, and yet I, too, have been often helped by this tiny piece of wisdom. Even now, when someone does something offensive or troubling, I sometimes find myself muttering under my breath, "his wife's giving birth in the backseat." It's one of the trim-tabs I use to keep my responses on an even keel.

## The Tongue as Rudder

Ultimately, it is the teaching of the Christian church that the cross and the resurrection together are the trim-tab events around which all of redemptive history turns, yet our *personal* histories often turn on what we do with our tongues, as the apostle James points out:

> Look at the ships: though they are so large that it takes strong winds to drive them, yet they are guided by a very small rudder wherever the will of the pilot directs. So also the tongue is a small member, yet it boasts of great exploits. (James 3:4-5)

It is with our tongues that we tell the tales, and with our tongues that we seal the secrets and maintain the silences. With our tongues we create the cycles of stories that make up the climate zones of the spiritual life of the church. Talk determines the cycles that, large and small, interconnect into an atmosphere—a huge, dynamic, moving, complex weather system of beliefs, images, habits of mind, relationships and disruptions in relationships, and accepted practices and taboos. Within this atmosphere we come to understand what it means to be Christian, what Christians believe, what we should do, how we should look, what we should not do, what we should aspire for, what we should be ashamed of, and where we should place our hope of redemption.

To this end, pastoral caregivers, parents, and kindly listening ears work to find the points of leverage that can help hurting people in our care into better, more faithful, and more Christian points of view. Often as we talk we listen for clues about what's really going on, the truths that cannot be said out loud, the issues lurking just out of sight behind the masks of adequacy, or rage, or withdrawal, or power, or perfectionism. Then we try to help people find the redemptive perspectives, the trim-tabs that will leverage everything into a more faithful framework.

Sometimes the leveraging has to do with honest confession and heartfelt repentance. Pastoral caregivers often wait for many hours, patiently building up trust until those who have come to them are able to say out loud the name of their inner shame. At moments like those, what the pastor may have to give may be a word of prayer, the offer of grace, or the declaration that God, too, has kept his promise to forgive. These are tiny moments, but moments that leverage life onto more faithful pathways.

So it is, in a striking parallel to Peter Senge's comments about trim-tabs on the rudders of ships, that apostle James tells us that the tongue, too, exerts enormous leverage, hopefully—if used in a Christian sense—as a vehicle of grace.

# "FOR THE LOVE OF GOD, MONTRESOR!"

## Grace for the Shadow Self

*The course of our life is determined . . . by an array of selves that live within each of us. These selves call out to us constantly—in our dreams and fantasies, in our moods and maladies, and in a multitude of unpredictable and inexplicable reactions to the world around us.*
—Hal Stone and Sidra Winkelman

In Edgar Allen Poe's short story, "A Cask of Amontillado," Montresor, the antagonist and narrator, tells a bone-chilling tale of luring an unsuspecting enemy—ironically named Fortunato—into the cellar of his mansion to sample a cask of fine amontillado wine. Before the story's end, Montresor has manacled Fortunato to the bulwark and calmly walled him in. What makes the matter bone chilling is the dispassionate, methodical way Montresor prepares for and delivers this act of revenge. He prepares the bricks and mortar in advance. He feigns friendship with Fortunato, plies him with wine, and invites him to the cellar in the dead of night. Even the diction of the narration is stripped of emotion, a haunting suggestion that Montresor has walled away more than an old enemy; he has systematically cut himself off from the horror of what he is doing.

In the terms we have been developing in this book, Fortunato is Montresor's Shadow, walled off and left to die in the cellar of his inner life. By the time the story closes, Fortunato is fully sober, but unable to move because of the manacles. He cries out from the pit, "For the love of God, Montresor!" but his cries are no longer heeded. As I prepared this manuscript I could not help thinking that we are all in some way both Montresor and Fortunato; each of us caught up in an effort of repression, walled off from the horror of what we are doing to our own inner lives. We need our Fortunato.

The purpose of this book has not been to solve the problem of the Shadow self; that's a matter for another study. My purpose here has been only to point out its presence, and to clarify its connections with the daily gossip on the one hand and our spiritual lives on the other. Even so, when I have spoken about this problem with classes of students at the university or in the church, I am often asked for help.

I am afraid that on one level, pastoral caregivers have to disappoint the earnest people who come to us. When they ask for "help," what they mean is that they want us to help them do away with the Shadow selves that trouble them so deeply. They want a fix, like the man who called me late one night and said in all seriousness, "My wife just left me after eleven years. Can you give me some Scriptures that will fix this problem?" "No," I told him, "the Bible isn't magic, and Christian faith isn't about quick fixes. It's taken you and your wife eleven years to destroy your marriage. Are you willing to give eleven years to putting it back together?" As my psychologist friend Roger Johnson sometimes says, "There are moments when you have to disappoint a client's wants in order to satisfy the client's needs."

But there's another reason pastoral caregivers are not able to fix their clients' Shadow selves: Clients need their Shadows. To be without a Shadow is to be broken and in need of fixing. Rather than a fix for the Shadow, what we need instead is to learn what it is and what it has to teach us.

## Everyone Has a Shadow

People who believe they have no Shadow are people without substance, or they are people who are afraid to step out into the light. As the apostle John says, "If we say that we have no sin, we deceive ourselves, and the truth is not in us" (1 John 1:8). Indeed, you can't develop a trait without also learning to managing its opposite. If we are to be people of discipline, we must learn to manage our laziness. If we are to be generous, we must learn to manage our greed. But the potential for laziness and greed remain within us, sneaking around in our subconscious selves, waiting for the chance to peek out from behind our masks of discipline and generosity. As psychologists Connie Zweig and Steve Wolf put it, "To face the best and the worst in our own natures is to live an authentic life." [1]

As we saw in chapter 7, learning to manage our Shadows is an important part of growing up. Part of what makes us human is our ability to choose what responses we will make to what happens to us, and to make those choices based on principles, values, and deep convictions. Yet, the presence of the Shadow sometimes trips up our efforts to act on our own best convictions.

One of the most puzzling aspects of human growth may be explained in terms of the inability to "face the best and the worst in our own natures." When people age, some grow more rigid and uptight, while others grow more mellow and accepting of life. Why is that? Carl Jung has suggested that the first half of life is spent learning the roles that go with the masks we wear, developing the split between the inner and the outer selves. But the second half of life carries the opposite challenge: To rediscover and reintegrate those aspects of the self that had been disowned during the early years.

It seems to me that people who do that well become more

accepting of life's ups and downs, more able to forgive flaws in others because they recognize those flaws in themselves, more tolerant of differences of opinion because they experience their own inner lives as varied and complex. People who do not come to terms with their own Shadows grow more rigid and inflexible because they have to invest increasing amounts of energy repressing the parts of the self that frighten them.

**Some of Our Greatest Strengths Are in the Shadow**

Not everything in the Shadow is sinful, or even something to be ashamed of. In fact, some of our greatest strengths and resources are character traits we have consigned to our Shadows.

It's important to remember that the daily business of gossip is a cultural process, not a particularly religious one, even when it comes packaged in religious language. This means that the impressions made on our minds by our parents' table talk were sometimes reflections of culture, not always the will of God. Sometimes we grow up ashamed of something, not because it is morally wrong, but because we heard our parents and friends say shameful things about it in their talk at the dinner table. But our parents and friends are not God, and their opinions do not have the force of Scripture or revealed truth.

Several years ago one of my graduate students was the owner of a successful business in Michigan. Every time I visited Peter he picked me up at the airport in a different Mercedes-Benz. He already held a Ph.D. in the field of pharmacology in which his business specialized. But later in life, after his father's death, he returned to school to study theology.

"All of this stuff was for my father," Peter told me. "I inherited the business from him. It would have broken his heart if he knew that I hated all of this. I don't care about the money. I want to pastor a church. And I'm going to, now that he's gone. I ran the business to satisfy him, I'm going to seminary to satisfy my own soul."

Peter's "confession" to me took no nerve because he knew I would honor his sense of vocation, but the fact that he waited until his father had died before he could follow the leading of his own heart is an indication of the depth of courage he would have had to draw upon if he were to tell his father these things. His yearning for ministry was stuffed deeply into his Shadow self.

## People Need Their Shadows to Be Whole

You need your whole self to be a whole person, including those parts of the self that make you uncomfortable, or that would have been problems for your parents. Perhaps this is most visible in the matter of what I will call "uncomfortable emotions," such as anger, grief, or envy. Christians have a particularly difficult time with uncomfortable emotions because of Paul's famous passage about the fruit of the spirit in Galatians 5:22-23:

> The fruit of the Spirit is love, joy, peace, patience, kindness, generosity, faithfulness, gentleness, and self-control. There is no law against such things."

In contrast, Paul lists the desires of the flesh:

> Fornication, impurity, licentiousness, idolatry, sorcery, enmities, strife, jealousy, anger, quarrels, dissentions, factions, envy, drunkenness, carousing, and things like these (vv. 19-21).

As we think about these verses as indications of the nature of sinfulness and holiness, we do well to remember that in this very letter, Paul himself expresses a seething anger at the "Judaizers" who would lead his Galatian converts into error:

> I am astonished that you are so quickly deserting the one who called you in the grace of Christ and are turning to a different gospel—not that there is another gospel, but there are some who are confusing you and want to pervert the gospel of Christ. But even if we or an angel from heaven should proclaim to you a gospel contrary to what we proclaimed to you, let that one be accursed! As we have said before, so now I repeat, if anyone proclaims to you a gospel contrary to what you received, let that one be accursed! (1:6-9)

Apparently Paul himself was able to tap deep reservoirs of anger when these were necessary for the defense of the gospel! The question is not whether we will be angry, but whether we will be angry at appropriate things, in appropriate degree, and whether we will express that anger in appropriate ways.

I learned the importance of appropriate anger from a conversation I once had with my son Jonathan. When Jonathan's older sister Michal Beth was regularly dancing ballet, we often carpooled to the studio with another family from our town. The other girl, whom I will call Bonnie, was a tall, rather gangling girl who was taking ballet to add a little grace to her daily movements. She stuttered terribly, and ballet was a perfect art form for her. On the way to class one day, Michal Beth and I taught Bonnie how to recite Robert Frost's poem, "Stopping by a Woods on a Snowy Evening." Before she got home, she could say the entire poem without stumbling over a single word.

She told us later what happened. When she got home she ran into the den and said to her father, "D-d-d-a-d-d-d-y. L-l-l-i-s-t-e-n t-t-o w-w-w-h-h-h-a-t-t-t I-I-I c-c-c-a-a-a-n-n-n s-s-s-a-y," and then she repeated the whole poem, word for word, without a stutter.

Bonnie's father looked at her and said, as only such a man can say, "Why would anybody waste any time on a stupid thing like that?"

The point of this recitation lies in Jonathan's reaction when I told him what Bonnie's father had said to her. He was instantly incensed. "Daddy," he said, "if humanity is a swimming pool with a deep end and a shallow end, that man's humanity isn't even a splash on the sidewalk." His eyes flashed, and his words choked in his throat.

"You're really angry," I said. I had never seen him so angry.

"Daddy," he said. "Sometimes you have to be angry. Sometimes anger is the right response, and if you're not angry, there's something wrong with you."

Gradually and somewhat painfully I have come to see that what I learned from Jonathan about anger is true of the other difficult emotions as well. We need our ability to be angry if we are going to seek justice. We need our ability to grieve if we are ever going to deal adequately with loss, or if we are to release loved ones to the past, or if we are to feel the grief of others. Envy, when it speaks to us, can be a wake-up call to re-explore the nature of blessedness. Even the uncomfortable emotional terrain of our Shadows can provide sources of strength and wisdom, but only if we can turn around and view it clearly.

## Sometimes Our Sinfulness Is a Symptom of Our Woundedness

Sometimes even the sinful things we do should be treated as symptoms of deeper wounds and hurts in need of healing. I learned this lesson from a student named Gary. Gary was a ministerial student, quiet, thoughtful, sometimes a little awkward socially. One evening he stayed late after class. I sensed from his demeanor that he was waiting for the room to clear. He filled the wait with chatter about this and that. Finally, when we were alone, he cleared his throat.

"Can we talk?" he said.

"Sure. What's up?" I replied.

"I have a problem with pornography,"

"That sounds really awful. Wanna get some coffee?"

As we talked, Gary showed me a part of his Shadow self that had become extraordinarily difficult for him to deal with. He watched me closely to see if I was going to "throw him under the bus," as my friend Peter St. Don says.

Gary's story astonished me. He was the son of a prominent minister in a large Midwestern city. One night when he was thirteen-years-old he was molested by an elder in his father's church. Rather than raise a public spectacle with an accusation, his father had taken the tack of saying nothing. To keep Gary safe, he had sent him away to a boarding school.

At the boarding school, Gary found himself wondering about his masculinity and his sexual orientation. Would his experience of having been molested by a man now turn him homosexual? It was a question he could not ask his father. Homosexuality was a taboo subject in his father's church, and he was afraid that perhaps his father had sent him away because he was ashamed of him. His strategy for answering his question about his sexual orientation was to turn to pornography.

My suspicion is that Gary's addiction to pornography was a way of self-medicating his sense of loss at having been abandoned by his father. The pornography was sinful, but the underlying psychological dynamics of his addiction required something beyond confession. He needed not only forgiveness, but healing. Without that healing, he would repeat this behavior over and over again. But of course, this is only one example. Any pastoral caregiver could provide others. Whatever its source, the shame attached to Gary's sinful behavior also kept him from dealing with the wound behind it. Gary's Shadow self had its own sustaining dynamic.

## And in the End . . . Grace

Finally, all of the readers of this book—Christian or not—remain in need of the radical grace of forgiveness for things we have done, or for what we have failed to do, or for things we have become, or for our open rebellion against God. Were it not for grace, this would be perhaps the most demoralizing thing I could have said, but I have listed it here as a point of encouragement because the grace we so desperately need is indeed a reality. The reality of grace is the most astonishing and wonderful fact in the whole of creation, the trim-tab on which the depth of our humanity turns. We have that reality, not as a matter of language or theory, but of granite hard fact. In the story of Jesus we encounter grace, freely, and fully given. It is a story that asks us also to be gracious in God's name—gracious to the strangers in our midst, but also no less gracious to the strangers who are our Shadow selves.

## NOTES

### Preface

1. John Cowan, *Small Decencies: Reflections and Meditations on Being Human at Work* (San Francisco: HarperCollins, 1992), 29.

2. Ibid., 33-4.

3. Jack Levin and Arnold Arluke, *Gossip: The Inside Scoop* (NewYork: Plenum Press, 1987), 18-9.

4. Matthew 13:24-30, 36-43.

5. John Sabini and Maury Silver, *Moralities of Everyday Life* (Oxford: Oxford University Press, 1982), 100-6.

6. Tex Sample, *Ministry in an Oral Culture: Living with Will Rogers, Uncle Remus and Minnie Pearl* (Louisville, Ky.: Westminster/John Knox, 1994), 68.

### Chapter 1

1. E. F. Schumacher, *A Guide for the Perplexed* (New York: Harper & Row, 1977), 1.

2. Tex Sample, *Ministry in an Oral Culture: Living with Will Rogers, Uncle Remus, and Minnie Pearl* (Louisville, Ky.: Westminster/John Knox, 1994).

3. John Sabini and Maury Silver, *Moralities of Everyday Life* (Oxford: Oxford University Press, 1982), 100-1.

4. In its enduring conversation about the role of the laity, the church has sometimes reinforced this dichotomy. For an excellent summary see Elizabeth Dreyer, *Earth Crammed with Heaven: A Spirituality of Everday Life* (Mahwah, N.J.: Paulist Press, 1994), 20-33.

5. I am often asked what I said in response. The answer is this: I said nothing at all. I went and sat beside her in her pew, I put my arm around her, and I cried.

6. Peter Berger, *A Rumor of Angels: Modern Society and the Rediscovery of the Supernatural* (Garden City, N.J.: Anchor Books, 1990).

### Chapter 2

1. This story is told as part of Craddock's tape series, "Storytelling and Preaching."

2. Edward Sapir, "Language," *Encyclopedia of the Social Sciences* (New York: Macmillan, 1933). This essay is also found in D. G. Mandelbaum, ed., *Culture, Language and Personality: Selected Writings of Edward Sapir* (Berkeley, Calif.: University of California Press, 1957), 7-32.

3. Peter Farb, *Word Play: What Happens When People Talk* (Toronto: Bantam Books, 1973), 62-3.

4. Judi Culbertson and Patti Bard, *Games Christians Play: An Irreverent Guide to Religion Without Tears* (New York: Harper & Row, 1967), 37-8.

5. D. J. Butler, "I Will Change Your Name," *We Exalt Your Name/Holiness Unto the Lord* (Vineyard Music Group, 1997), © 1987 Mercy/Vineyard Publishing (ASCAP). All rights reserved. Used with permission.

## Chapter 3

1. Neil Postman, *Amusing Ourselves to Death: Public Discourse in the Age of Show Business* (New York: Penguin Books, 1985), 7.

2. D. R. Dooling and R. Lachman, "Effects of Comprehension on Retention of Prose," *Journal of Experimental Psychology* 88 (1971): 216-22.

3. For this little rhetorical bit of gap-filling, I have to admit my debt to Salmon Rushdie, *The Moor's Last Sigh* (New York: Pantheon, 1995), 89.

4. A. Sanford and S. Garrod, *Understanding Written Language* (London: Wiley, 1981), 114.

5. Charles C. Fries, *Teaching and Learning English as a Foreign Language* (Ann Arbor: University of Michigan Press, 1945), 40.

6. I deal with these various features of language in a different book. See Jerry Camery-Hoggatt, *Speaking of God: Reading and Preaching the Word of God* (Peabody, Mass.: Hendrickson, 1995), esp. 47-160.

7. Stephen Crites, "The Narrative Quality of Experience," in *Why Narrative? Readings in Narrative Theology*, eds. Stanley Hauerwas and Gregory Jones (Grand Rapids, Mich.: Eerdmans, 1989), 71.

8. Thomas Moore, *Care of the Soul: A Guide for Cultivating Depth and Sacredness in Everyday Life* (New York: HarperCollins, 1992), 47.

9. Daniel Taylor, *The Healing Power of Stories: Creating Yourself Through the Stories of Your Life* (New York: Doubleday, 1996), 15.

10. Ibid., 21.

## Chapter 4

1. See Joshua Fishman, *Advances in the Sociology of Language* (The Hague: Mouton, 1971), 21-2.

2. Gerhard Lohfink, *The Bible: Now I Get It!* (New York, Doubleday, 1979), 24-5.

3. John Sabini and Maury Silber, *Moralities of Everyday Life* (Oxford: Oxford University Press, 1982), 98-9.

## Chapter 5

1. The full text of this story is found in David Reynolds, *Playing Ball on Running Water: The Japanese Way to Building a Better Life* (New York: Quill, 1984), 146-9. This version is an adaptation of that one.

2. Jack Handey, *Deepest Thoughts: So Deep They Squeak* (New York: Hyperion, 1994), pages not numbered.

3. For a much more extensive treatment of this process, see Jerry Camery-Hoggatt, *Speaking of God: Reading and Preaching the Word of God* (Peabody, Mass.: Hendrickson, 1992), 59-73.

4. Northrup Frye, *The Great Code: The Bible and Literature* (Toronto: Academic Press, 1981), 218.

5. Ibid.

6. George Lakoff and Mark Johnson, *Metaphors We Live By* (Chicago: University of Chicago Press, 1980), 3.

7. Ibid., 5.

8. Ray Bakke, *The Urban Christian: Effective Ministry in Today's Urban World* (Downers Grove, Ill.: InterVarsity, 1987), 20-1.

## Chapter 6

1. Stephen Covey, *The Seven Habits of Highly Successful People: Restoring the Character Ethic* (New York: Simon and Schuster, 1989), 30-1.

2. Sharon Parks, "Love Tenderly . . ." from *To Act Justly, Love Tenderly, Walk Humbly: An Agenda for Ministers,* by Walter Breuggemann, Sharon Parks, and Thomas Groome (New York: Paulist Press, 1986), 29-30.

3. Ibid.

## Chapter 7

1. Margaret Wise Brown, *Goodnight Moon* (New York: Harper & Row, 1947).

2. For this quote I am indebted to Jane Thompkins, *Reader-Response Criticism: From Formalism to Post-Structuralism* (Baltimore: Johns Hopkins University Press, 1980), xiv.

3. Bruno Bettelheim, *The Uses of Enchantment: The Meaning and Importance of Fairy Tales* (New York: Alfred Knopf, 1976), 4.

4. Ibid.

5. Ibid., 5.

6. Ibid., 85.

7. Ibid.

8. I might here point out that a number of theorists have recently explored the significance of this integration. Perhaps most to our point is Robert Bly's book, *Iron John* (Reading, Mass.: Addison-Wesley, 1990). *Iron John* has generated enormous interest because of its insistence that the child must not lose, but must come to terms with, the fiercer, shaggier, less manageable side of the psyche. Indeed, says Bly, a major problem in Western culture is that we have lost both the narrative tradition and the rituals by which young men can come to terms with this Wild Man who dwells in the darker side of the self (p. 15). The result is that we do not know how to be *fierce* any more.

## Chapter 8

1. In the comics the character was named Robert Bruce Banner, often reduced to Bruce.

2. Nathaniel Brandon, *The Disowned Self* (New York: Bantam Books, 1971), 8.

3. Erving Goffman, *Stigma: Notes on the Management of Spoiled Identity* (Englewood Cliffs, N.J.: Prentice-Hall, 1963), 73-91.

## Chapter 9

1. Daniel Goleman, *Vital Lies, Simple Truths: The Psychology of Self-Deception* (New York: Simon and Schuster, 1985), 17.

2. Arthur Miller, *The Crucible* (New York: Bantam, 1953), 5-6.

3. Michael Kelly Blanchard, "Cootie Girl," *Be Ye Glad Album* © 1986 New Spring Publishing, Inc. (ASCAP) (a div. of Brentwood-Benson Music Publishing Inc.) / Gotz Music (ASCAP) (admin. by The Copyright Company, Nashville, Tenn.). All rights reserved. Used by permission.

4. William Styron, *Sophie's Choice* (New York: Random House, 1976), 483-4.

## Chapter 10

1. Gershen Kaufman, *Shame: The Power of Caring* (Rochester, Ver.: Swchenken Books, 1992). Because the discussion that follows uses Kaufman's vocabulary, we should be clear that he is not discussing the Shadow itself. What we have in view is the *feelings we have toward the Shadow*, especially the sense of shame that comes over us when our Shadows feel exposed or threatened in some way.

2. John Patton, *Is Human Forgiveness Possible? A Pastoral Care Perspective* (Nashville: Abingdon, 1985), 20-1.

3. Ibid., 75.

4. Hanna Arendt, *The Human Condition* (Chicago: University of Chicago Press, 1958), 237.

5. Sallie Tisdale, "The Weight That Women Carry: the Compulsion to Diet in a Starved Culture," in *Minding the Body: Women Writers on Body and Soul*, ed. Patricia Foster (New York: Doubleday, 1994), 16.

## Chapter 11

1. Ronald Rolheiser, *The Holy Longing: The Search for a Christian Spirituality* (New York: Doubleday, 1999), 52.

2. Ibid.

3. Ibid., 59.

4. Karl Olsson, *Come to the Party: An Invitation to a Freer Lifestyle* (Waco, Tex.: Word, 1972), 18-9.

5. Victor Hugo, *Les Miserables* (New York: Modern Library, n.d.), 90.

6. Nathaniel Brandon, *The Disowned Self* (New York: Bantam Books, 1971), 60.

7. Olsson, *Come to the Party*, 46-7.

## Chapter 12

1. Peter Senge, *The Fifth Discipline: The Art and Practice of the Learning Organization* (New York: Doubleday, 1990), 64-5.

2. Ibid.

3. Ibid., 63.

4. Ibid., 7.

## Chapter 13

1. Connie Zweig and Stephen Wolf, *Romancing the Shadow* (New York: Ballantine Books, 1997), 8.

# BIBLIOGRAPHY


Arendt, Hanna. *The Human Condition*. Chicago: University of Chicago Press, 1958.

Bakke, Ray. *The Urban Christian: Effective Ministry in Today's Urban World*. Downers Grove, Ill.: InterVarsity, 1987.

Bettelheim, Bruno. *The Uses of Enchantment: The Meaning and Importance of Fairy Tales*. New York: Alfred Knopf, 1976.

Bly, Robert. *Iron John*. Reading, Mass.: Addison-Wesley, 1990.

Brandon, Nathaniel. *The Disowned Self*. New York: Bantam Books, 1971.

Brown, Margaret Wise. *Goodnight Moon*. New York: Harper & Row, 1947.

Breuggemann, Walter, Sharon Parks, and Thomas Groome. *Act Justly, Love Tenderly, Walk Humbly: An Agenda for Ministers*. New York: Paulist Press, 1986.

Camery-Hoggatt, Jerry. *Speaking of God: Reading and Preaching the Word of God*. Peabody, Mass.: Hendrickson, 1995.

Covey, Stephen. *The Seven Habits of Highly Effective People: Restoring the Character Ethic*. New York: Simon and Schuster, 1989.

Culbertson, Judi and Patti Bard. *Games Christians Play: An Irreverent Guide to Religion Without Tears*. New York: Harper & Row, 1967.

Dooling, D. R. and R. Lachman. "Effects of Comprehension on Retention of Prose." *Journal of Experimental Psychology* 88 (1971): 216-22.

Dreyer, Elizabeth. *Earth Crammed with Heaven: A Spirituality of Everyday Life*. Mahwah, N.J.: Paulist Press, 1994.

Evans, Jamie. *Uncommon Gifts: Transforming Learning Disabilities into Blessings*. Wheaton, Ill.: Harold Shaw, 1998.

Farb, Peter. *Word Play: What Happens When People Talk.* Toronto: Bantam Books, 1973.

Fishman, Joshua. *Advances in the Sociology of Language.* The Hague: Mouton, 1971.

Fries, Charles. *Teaching and Learning English as a Foreign Language.* Ann Arbor: University of Michigan Press, 1945.

Frye, Northrup. *The Great Code: The Bible and Literature.* Toronto: Academic Press, 1981.

Patricia Foster, ed. *Minding the Body: Women Writers on Body and Soul.* New York: Doubleday, 1994.

Gilkey, Langdon. *Shantung Compound.* New York: Harper & Row, 1966.

Goffman, Erving. *Stigma: Notes on the Management of Spoiled Identity.* Englewood Cliffs, N.J.: Prentice-Hall, 1963.

Goleman, Daniel. *Vital Lies, Simple Truths: The Psychology of Self-Deception.* New York: Simon and Schuster, 1985.

Handey, Jack. *Deepest Thoughts: So Deep They Squeak.* New York: Hyperion, 1994.

Hauerwas, Stanley and Gregory Jones, eds. *Why Narrative? Readings in Narrative Theology.* Grand Rapids, Mich.: Eerdmans, 1989.

Howard, Thomas. *Christ the Tiger.* Philadelphia: Lippincott, 1967.

Hugo, Victor. *Les Miserables.* New York: Modern Library, n.d.

Kaufman, Gershen. *Shame: The Power of Caring.* Rochester, Ver.: Schenkman Books, 1992.

Kegan, Robert. *The Evolving Self: Problem and Process in Human Development.* Cambridge, Mass.: Harvard University Press, 1982.

Lakoff, George and Mark Johnson. *Metaphors We Live By.* Chicago: University of Chicago Press, 1980.

Lohfink, Gerhard. *The Bible: Now I Get It!* New York: Doubleday, 1979.

Moore, Thomas. *Care of the Soul: A Guide for Cultivating Depth and Sacredness in Everyday Life.* New York: HarperCollins, 1992.

Myers, David G. *The Inflated Self: Human Illusions and the*

*Biblical Call to Hope*. New York: Seabury, 1980.

Olsson, Karl. *Come to the Party: An Invitation to a Freer Lifestyle*. Waco, Tex.: Word, 1972.

Patton, John. *Is Human Forgiveness Possible? A Pastoral Care Perspective*. Nashville: Abingdon, 1985.

Postman, Neil. *Amusing Ourselves to Death: Public Discourse in the Age of Show Business*. New York: Penguin Books, 1985.

Reynolds, David. *Playing Ball on Running Water: The Japanese Way to Building a Better Life*. New York: Quill, 1984.

Rolheiser, Ronald. *The Holy Longing: The Search for a Christian Spirituality*. New York: Doubleday, 1999.

Sabini, John and Maury Silver. *Moralities of Everyday Life*. Oxford: Oxford University Press, 1982.

Sample, Tex. *Ministry in an Oral Culture: Living with Will Rogers, Uncle Remus, and Minnie Pearl*. Louisville, Ky.: Westminster/John Knox, 1994.

Sanford, A. and S. Garrod. *Understanding Written Language*. London: Wiley, 1981.

Schumacher, E. F. *A Guide for the Perplexed*. New York: Harper & Row, 1977.

Senge, Peter. *The Fifth Discipline: The Art and Practice of the Learning Organization*. New York: Doubleday, 1990.

Styron, William. *Sophie's Choice*. New York: Random House, 1976.

Taylor, Daniel. *The Healing Power of Stories: Creating Yourself Through the Stories of Your Life*. New York: Doubleday, 1996.

Thompkins, Jane. *Reader-Response Criticism: From Formalism to Post-Structuralism*. Baltimore: Johns Hopkins University Press, 1980.

Zweig, Connie and Stephen Wolf. *Romancing the Shadow*. New York: Ballantine Books, 1997.

## THE AUTHOR

JOHN BLOM

Jerry Camery-Hoggatt is professor of New Testament and Narrative Theology at Vanguard University of Southern California. He is the author of several books on the Gospel of Mark and other concerns related to the interpretation of the Bible.